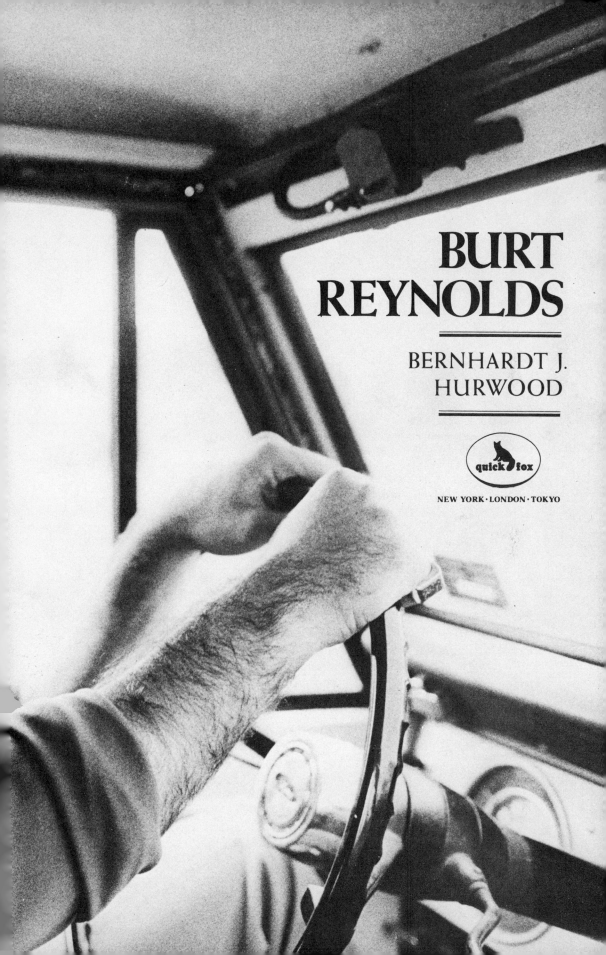

# BURT REYNOLDS

BERNHARDT J.
HURWOOD

quick fox

NEW YORK · LONDON · TOKYO

# Photo Credits

Ulvis Alberts (pages 1, 40, 64-65);
Peter Borsari/Camera 5 (page 98);
Audrey Chiu/Michelson Agency
(pages 8, 12-13, 16, 36, 46-47, 70); Bill
Holz/Michelson Agency (pages 6, 42,
56-57, 66-67, 72, 74, 76, 88, 95, 111); Al
Satterwhite/Camera 5 (pages 2-3, 5,
96, 99, 100); United Press International (pages 11, 15, 24, 29, 32-33,
34, 39, 44, 48, 50, 52, 58, 59, 60-61, 63,
82-83, 87, 90-91, 92, 93, 94, 102, 108);
Errol Waltzer/Michelson Agency
(pages 9, 14, 68-69, 71); Warner Bros.
(page 89); Wide World Photos (pages
10, 21 top and bottom, 22, 26, 30-31,
54, 78, 81, 85, 86, 104).

Designed by Frances Greenberg

Front cover photograph by
Ron Galella

Back cover photograph by
Al Satterwhite

Copyright © Quick Fox, 1979

All rights reserved.

Printed in the United States of
America.

International Standard Book
Number: 0-8256-3942-5
Library of Congress Catalog Card
Number: 79-90893

In Great Britian: Book Sales Ltd.,
　　　　　　　　78 Newman Street,
　　　　　　　　London W1P 3LA.

In Canada: Gage Trade Publishing,
　　　　　　P.O. Box 5000, 164 Com-
　　　　　　mander Blvd., Agincourt,
　　　　　　Ontario M1S 3C7.

In Japan: Quick Fox, 4-26-22 Jin-
　　　　　gumae, Shibuya-ku, Tokyo
　　　　　150.

# O N E

# THE IMAGE, THE EXPERTS, AND THE MAN

In the old days, superstars were the composite creations of big Hollywood studio hypesters working in close cooperation with gossip columnists. Rarely, if ever, did the superstar have anything to do with his or her own creation. But that was the way things were in the old days.

Today, Burt Reynolds is the outstanding example of a superstar who has "made" himself. Furthermore, he is a "mass of contradictions," as the well-known celebrity-watcher Claire Safran wrote. She pointed out that he is "a sex symbol who doesn't believe in fooling around, a *machismo* figure who is bored by hunting, and who hasn't shot anything 'since I read *Bambi*.' An avid reader whose bookshelves hold a well-thumbed copy of *Paradise Lost* and a smattering of hardcore pornography. A former football star who now prefers word games to almost any other kind."

Bob Lardine of the New York *Daily News* sized Burt up this way: "At one time, he had a reputation for being a short-tempered, one-fisted drinker. He kept the other fist ready to belt out any offending pest." Lardine went on to observe that Burt Reynolds was a changed man, that he was, "witty, charming and articulate … a teetotaler … who would rather engage in a fierce game of charades with pals Mel Brooks, Norman Fell and Dom DeLuise than smack an ill-mannered interviewer in the mouth."

Betty White, writing for *The Saturday Evening Post* had this to say, "Burt Reynolds is an actor. If you think he is the good old boy who strides through his mostly less-than-memorable movies with a lewd wink and a ready fist, you're wrong. Or if he is the good old boy, he can do a very convincing interpretation of an intelligent, thoughtful man who is willing to take chances in order to grow. Take your pick. I think it's harder to fake brains than brawn."

7

Clearly the experts recognize that what you see isn't necessarily what you're looking at. What they are saying about Burt Reynolds is that the public figure, if not exactly a fictional character, is certainly a thoughtfully constructed one. They are saying that here is one very smart cookie who has succeeded in blending the hype with reality and has managed to have a good time in the process.

The matter of technique was pointed out in the *New Yorker* by critic Pauline Kael, who explained: "Burt Reynolds, the only actor to have reached stardom via the talk shows, is also the first movie star to make a *style* out of his awareness of the audience's response to him as an off-screen celebrity....Burt Reynolds has become popular by letting the public see his insider's jokey contempt for the whole entertainment business.... He showed an amazingly fast, spangly put-down wit, but he also showed something else...he made a joke of the profession. He came on as a man who had no higher values than the buck and the pleasures of the flesh — exactly what many people in the audience had always really believed stardom was about. His message was that stars were just bums, and that he himself was an honest, funny bum—too smart and too gamy to give much of a damn about anything except having a good time, and too cocky to lie about it. His message was that he was having a ball being a celebrity."

Recently, however, now that he is getting older and wiser, Burt Reynolds has been shedding some of the *machismo* and permitting the real man to emerge. "There are people who think I crawled out from under some magazine cover," he observes, with a twinkle in his eye. Then becoming serious he adds: "I don't have much regard for the kind of person I've been made out to be, you know, a movie star swinger who tells his girl to be dressed and outta here by 5:00 A.M."

*With Sally Fields en route to Alabama*

H aving recently opened his own successful dinner theatre, in Jupiter, Florida, his home town, Burt Reynolds has been doing a lot more than acting. Most interesting, perhaps "revealing" would be a better word, was an interview in Jupiter that appeared on the NBC "Today Show" on May 1, 1979.

In the interview, Reynolds commented: "There's a reason why Pacino and DeNiro — that a lot of people think they're the same guy. There's a reason for that. They don't show themselves. They don't make themselves available. They don't stick their chins out and say, 'Here's who I am. I'm an actor, and that's all I'm going to give you, that portion of me.' Well, when you start sticking your chin out, and making yourself available, and becoming a public person, a personality as it were, what happens is that the actor is suddenly pushed over to the side and the actor is never going to be given the amount of credit he should be given, because the personality takes over."

"Did this happen to you?" he was asked.

"I know it's happened to me," he replied emphatically.

The interviewer commented, "I keep reading that you want to break out of this role that a lot of peole have you in, as a kind of good ole boy, who's usually seen in films making U-turns at 85 miles per hour. Why do you want to do that? Those are important roles."

Burt sighed. "What I want to do is use every one of the tools I think I have as an actor that I've worked for 22 years to get....And I feel that there's what I call the constipated school of acting—I'm sorry, but that's what I call it. Every year that get an Academy Award nomination and a tube of Preparation H. And then I feel that there's that school of acting I call the 'Cary Grant school of acting,' which is

*Burt's Cadillac*

so absolutely wonderful that people say, 'He shouldn't be nominated. It's too easy, what he does.' I work *so hard* to make it look easy that I'm afraid I've kind of been overlooked a few times."

"Does it bother you?"

"Yeah, it bothers me."

"Henry Fonda never won an Academy Award, and he's a premier actor. Why is it that important?"

Burt shifted in his seat and replied, "It's not important to win an Academy Award. It's important that you be recognized, and Fonda is recognized as one of the really fine American actors living today. I would like to be given credit for creating this character, this fellow [the public Burt Reynolds], whether you like him or not. Somebody must like him because the pictures are doing fairly well,

*Barbara Walters interviews Burt*

and I like him. Again I keep saying, I'm having fun with him, but I would like to stretch him out a little bit. And the way to do that is first of all to have the words. Those are the most important things. The words.

"I just did a film called *Starting Over*, which is an appropriate title for that film because it is kind of starting over for me. It's about a guy who's in his forties and just gets divorced, and midlife crisis, etc., etc. And it's a real stretch for me. It's going to be interesting to see if the people who have followed me and cared about me in spite of what they've read, or whatever, if they go to see that film — and if they'll like me in that kind of picture, because I don't drive over 35 miles per hour."

"But you've tried that kind of picture before and it hasn't been very commercially successful in the past."

*Jaye P. Morgan with Burt on the TV special "Burt and the Girls," 1973*

"That's not true," Burt Reynolds replied emphatically. "I tried it in *The End* and *The End* was very successful. The picture was made for $2 million. I produced it and directed it, and so far it's made over $20 million. That's successful."

For Burt Reynolds, however, a $20 million gross is no big deal. Consider his immensely popular *Smokey and the Bandit*. A relative turkey in the high-rise urban areas, especially in the northeast, *Smokey* was a runaway smash in CB country, which included just about all the rest of the United States. So far, *Smokey* has grossed somewhere in the neighborhood of $100 million — that's a tenth of a billion — and Burt is raking in 20% of the profits.

Just mention the picture to him and he just breaks out into something that resembles a walking smile button. He says, "Every single one of my advisors and friends went down on their hands and knees begging me with tears in their eyes not to make that film. Mind you, if you had read the original script, you'd probably have done the same. The truth is I ad libbed almost every line."

What it all boils down to is that Burt knows what he wants. He's stubborn when his gut instinct tells him that he's right, but he isn't pigheaded and he knows that giving in when the other guy is right does not constitute defeat. He is no less tough than he was back in his angry, chip-on-the-shoulder days, but he isn't ashamed of letting his sensitivity show. He still has a quick temper, and has no qualms about blowing his stack. On the other hand he doesn't make hasty decisions. He has managed to achieve a practical blend of cynicism and idealism.

On the business of the image, he's never lost sight of his perspective, observing, "It can get downright dangerous for yourself if you begin to believe the studio hype. Someday you may just throw yourself against a brick wall, forgetting that it's not a breakaway."

*With Kristy McNichol in* The End

# T W O

# OLE
# BUDDY

**B**urt Reynolds was born in Waycross, Georgia, on February 11, 1936. From the moment he began to toddle, the family started calling him Buddy to avoid confusion with his father, also named Burt. Even as a child, the younger Reynolds was not the type to be called "Junior."

His mother's side of the family was predominantly Italian, and his father, a former cowboy, was half Cherokee. Commenting on his ethnic background with the usual flip manner that fans have come to appreciate, Burt once said, "With my mother being Italian and my father being Indian, my confusion is simple — one-half of me wants to grow hair and the other half doesn't."

The family moved to Riviera Beach on Florida's gold coast and settled down in a neighborhood made up predominantly of fishermen. Consequently he spent a lot of time fishing, exploring the Everglades with the other kids, and not infrequently getting into scrapes. "I was a wild kid," he recalls. "Restless and rebellious. My Dad was police chief of West Palm Beach and somehow that made me resentful. He really didn't have a dangerous job. Most of his calls were for things like, 'Mrs. Dodge can't get her garage door open.' The thing that kept my feet on the ground was athletics, especially football."

There was only one thing that bothered young Buddy. He was constantly being pushed into proving his masculinity by other kids. They called him "Mullet," a slur on the working-class neighborhood in which he lived, or "Greaseball," a nasty crack at his ancestry. Consequently, he rarely turned down a dare or a challenge to fight when the gauntlet was tossed at him.

But even at that age he had a sense of compassion and a feeling for others. One day he brought home one of his best friends after seeing what abominable conditions the boy lived in. Jim never left, and from that day on Buddy and his sister, Nancy, had a new brother. Obviously, that also speaks well for the senior members of the Reynolds family, for their capacity to give love and affection.

Unfortunately for Buddy, his father was not a demonstrative man. "Going to hug him," Burt recalls today, "was like trying to hug a statue of Lincoln. You just didn't....My whole family was undemonstrative. My mother, my brother and sister and I — we never touched each other or expressed our affection."

**B**etween the cool atmosphere of disciplined no nonsense at home and the continuous need to be defensive at school the pressure finally built up to the breaking point. When he was 15 Buddy Reynolds ran away, determined to make his way in the world alone. Very quickly he discovered what the outside world was like. Although he managed to make it all the way to South Carolina, he was arrested for vagrancy and sentenced to serve a week on a chain gang as a water boy. Since he was a juvenile, after that the authorities sent him back to West Palm Beach. But the fresh recollections of his stern, no-nonsense home life, which included parental corporal punishment, only bolstered Buddy's determination. Instead of going home he went to live at the house of his girlfriend.

Actually he was hoping for some sign of acceptance from his father. He wanted to be asked to come home. He would even have been happy if he had been ordered to return. But both father and son were unbending and neither would give. When the two met on the street the elder Reynolds invariably greeted his son with a cool, "How are you, boy?" Looking back, Burt recalls, "I wanted to prove something to my father, but, of course I didn't. There's a saying in the South that you're not a man until your father tells you so." Buddy's father wasn't ready to tell him yet, and Buddy knew it, so he went home after a year.

Meanwhile, at Palm Beach High, Buddy plunged into athletics. "If I hadn't been a jock," he said, "I never would have finished high school. I was having a severe identity crisis. We didn't have any dope then, but if we had, I would've been into it. I'd try anything twice. I lived in what I thought was Rivera Beach, didn't know for years it was spelled Riviera. The kids from that section were called "mullets" and "greaseballs." I tried to play football, basketball, everything. One day I found out I could outrun everybody in the school. I scored a touchdown and they didn't call me "mullet" anymore. They were all saying, 'Hi, Buddy!' Amazing, isn't it? One day I was "mullet" and the next day I was Buddy In the back of my mind I thought, 'Boy! If there ever comes a time when you can't outrun everybody — if you don't score — you'll go back to being a mullet,' so you continue to run faster. And sometimes you don't run faster, you just run over That was my incentive to go to school."

**A**nd girls. In the early fifties the jock got the girl. Now it tears up my brother, who is a coach, to see some 220-pound high school kid with a guitar on his back, two joints in his pocket, and a girl in each hand. The kid will say, 'Why should I get killed playing football when it's easier to get what I want this way.'"

Burt grins when he remembers his first high school steady girl, the one he almost married. She was a bright-eyed brunette with a ready laugh and a quick tongue. "I was attracted to her body — I mean her personality," he recalls. "Her parents didn't approve of me, and I had to call for her at the service entrance. We used to drink Purple Passions and listen to 'The Great Pretender' in the back seat of her car."

She was succeeded by a whole procession of luscious young lovelies — a fledgling ballerina, an entire flock of stewardesses (before they became known as Flight Attendants), a platoon of secretaries, and a glittering cluster of starlets. He describes them all as being "independent, with a sense of humor and with their heads screwed on right." They were also all 3-dimensional knockouts with measurements guaranteed to stop traffic, or, as Burt put it, "chicks who would make eyes pop."

Burt's gridiron achievements as a high school jock stood him in good stead when he entered Florida State College. Not only did he get good grades, he soon became an All-Florida and All-Southern Conference running back. He attracted the attention of big league scouts, and was signed by the Baltimore Colts — all this while still an undergraduate. Then came the near-fatal accident that radically altered his career.

I t was Christmas Eve of his sophomore year at FSC. Somewhat carried away with his popularity, especially with the girls, and on the reckless side because of his father's position, Burt was a heavy-footed driver. Faster than almost anyone he knew on the football field, he found it hard to resist the impulse to beat everyone on the road when he was behind the wheel. Recalling that night with grim clarity, he says, "I was driving a big Buick and I got a ticket for doing 95 miles per hour. I remember looking at the speeding ticket in one hand and thinking how my father was going to beat the crap out of me."

Looking at a ticket, or anything else while you're driving at night is not a good idea. But Burt, having started driving again, and maintaining a fairly contrite 35, barely felt himself moving after his previous, breakneck 95. "Suddenly," he recalls, "I looked up and found myself headed for a flat-bed truck filled with cement blocks that was stretched across the road."

Slamming on the brakes he dived under the dashboard a split second before plowing into the truck and shearing off the top of the car. Burt was pinned in the wreckage. A man from the truck rushed over and peered nervously into the wreckage. "You in there!" he called. "Are y' still alive?"

"I'm hurt!" called Buddy. "I can't move...please, call my father, he's the chief of police!"

It was the worst thing he could have said. The truck, it turned out, was being loaded with stolen cement blocks. The man rushed back to his two accomplices and told them the bad news. Choosing discretion over Good Samaritanism, the three fled, leaving the hapless victim in the lap of the gods.

"I've always been lucky," observed Burt. Twenty minutes later a police car passed, came to a screeching halt, and radioed for help. It took 7 hours to cut him loose from the wreckage, and when they got to him he was scrunched up into a tight ball. It wasn't until they got him into the ambulance and straightened him out that he began to hemorrhage. A ruptured spleen notwithstanding, his blood had coagulated thereby preventing profuse bleeding. At the hospital they performed emergency surgery, during which they removed his spleen and patched up his knees as best they could. They had both been badly hurt, but one was

19

crushed. It meant the end of his football career. When he got over the physical part of the accident — he was in fabulous shape, and he healed quickly — Burt had to cope with the emotional shock. He quit school and headed for New York. It was almost like running away in a panic. "Once those knees were screwed up," he said, "I had to forget about playing pro ball."

But after hanging around New York for a while doing odd jobs like washing dishes at Schrafft's, he thought he had gotten his strength back and he decided to go back to school and try again. The dream of being a pro footballer didn't die easily. He deserved credit for trying, and the school authorities deserve it for giving him the chance, but it didn't work. He recalls, "I had only one good good wheel, and I was exactly one step slower. The hole would open, and I'd see myself going through it, but I wouldn't get there. So I quit school and went back to New York again. I was depressed, I was unhappy, I was drinking, in short, I was well on my way to becoming a bum."

How it happened, he doesn't know, but he started hanging out with actors in Greenwich Village. He also worked as a bouncer at Roseland. "I had no eyes to be an actor," he recalls. "I didn't know what they were talking about most of the time. Somebody asked me if I ever read *The Catcher in the Rye*. Hell, I was 21 years old, and I had never read any book at all, so I read *The Catcher in the Rye*, and I thought, hey, this is good. That book got me interested in reading, changed my life."

He goes on to say, "I was running around with Rip Torn, who's one of the best actors in the world, and a very physical guy. I'd play basketball with him at the "Y" and he'd wipe me out. He had tremendous drive that he used in his acting. I had no place to put my drive."

When he talks about this period of his life he chuckles sometimes, especially when he hearkens back to the incident revolving around *The Catcher in the Rye*. When pressed for details he says, "I bumped into this guy at a bar and he asked me if I could read. I almost slugged him. What he meant, of course, was could I read lines. He was a writer."

The writer was Conrad Hopkins, now an English professor, but he and Burt became friendly, and Hopkins got the young ex-jock interested in books and plays. Being no dummy, Burt decided to go about it sensibly. He went back to Florida to study drama at Palm Beach Junior College after Hopkins had arranged for him to get a taste of theatre at the Hyde Park Playhouse on Long Island.

In Palm Beach in 1958, his performance in a school production of *Outward Bound* won him the Florida Drama Award and a scholarship to, of all places, the Hyde Park Playhouse. So it was back to New York. While he was an apprentice there, Joanne Woodward came out during the summer to play a leading role in one of the playhouse productions. Looking back, Burt says, "I was an apprentice and she was a star, but she helped me secure my very first agent so I could get some real jobs."

Describing Burt's meeting with Joanne Woodward in *The Saturday Evening Post*, Betty White wrote, "...she thought he was just the nicest person that she'd met in a long time. So she introduced him to her agent and the agent signed him

*(top) Rehearsing a scene for "The Twilight Zone," 1963 ; (bottom) A 1959 comparison of Burt's resemblance to Marlon Brando*

*Burt as he appeared in "Riverboat"*

Betty White asked Burt: "Was it because of your talent or your looks?"

Burt replied, "Well, it certainly wasn't my talent. I did look like Marlon Brando, but I think it was because Joanne just took an interest in this shy person who was always peering around the curtains....I first met Joanne, I was so shy that I carried my lunch in a paper bag so I could hide somewhere at lunchtime."

The first jobs were no beds of roses. "For a TV show named 'Frontiers of Faith,'" Burt reminisces, "there was a bit that called for a guy to be thrown through a window. I did it and got paid something like $132. I thought it was terrific. After that I did a lot of TV. When a script called for a guy to get thrown through a window or down the stairs, I got the part. There were no stunt men because TV was live. I'd say three lines and get knocked down. As the years went by I began getting knocked down less and talking more."

Burt is the first one to remind interviewers that he had to work to get where he was, and that he was fortunate to be encouraged by others. About the actors he met before he really got started, he admits that he had preconceptions and that he abandoned them.

"I found they were not at all the way I expected them to be," he commented. "They weren't all gay, they weren't all interested only in themselves. They encouraged me to try acting, as my literature teacher had once suggested.... People would like to think that I was an overnight success, but I paid my dues. I spent 2 years doing theatre in the East before I became a talking body on TV."

Burt made his New York theatrical debut in a City Center revival of *Mr. Roberts*, starring Charlton Heston, and he admits to being very impressed. *The Ten Commandments* was still playing its first run at the Criterion Theatre on Broadway, and Heston, who played Moses, was regarded very much with awe.

Recalling his role as Seaman Mannion in *Mr. Roberts*, Burt said about the production, "It had a great cast with Charlton Heston in the lead. John Forsythe was in it. I'll never forget when I looked up and there stood 'Moses' in the doorway. I looked at Heston standing there enormous in his topcoat and I thought, *I'll never be able to call him Chuck*. Then he took three steps into the room, tripped, and fell flat on the floor. And that's how I met my first big movie star."

In 1959, Los Angeles began edging New York out as the television capital of the U.S. It was the beginning of a mass exodus which included actors, directors, producers, writers, technicians, and wide-eyed aspirants to the glamorous life. Burt Reynolds went also. "When all the agents moved West, so did I," he noted.

*Burt as "Hawk"*

# T H R E E

# EARLY HOLLYWOOD - TV DAYS

**B**urt Reynolds made his official television debut while still in the cast of *Mr. Roberts* at the New York City Center. He was given a guest star role in the TV series, "M Squad," which starred Lee Marvin. For a young actor in the early stages of his career, it was a feather in the cap. Burt had a lot going for him, though. He was a good-looking former football player. He was 27 years old, and as far as his future was concerned, the prognosis was excellent, although he probably did not realize it at the time. It had strictly to do with who was behind him. He was being represented by MCA, which today is a mammoth entertainment conglomerate that is the parent company of Universal Pictures, among others. At the time, however, MCA was one of the most influential talent agencies in the business.

Shortly after arriving on the West Coast, Burt got his first big break. He recalls, "I'd been in Hollywood only a few months when suddenly I got this series. Lew Wasserman [president of MCA] had brought me out from New York and told people I was going to be a big star. You know what that means at MCA—if Lew Wasserman says it's going to rain, everybody puts up an umbrella. I was a green kid so far as the film industry was concerned."

Burt was then signed by Review Productions as the young river pilot, Ben Frazer, in "Riverboat," an hour-long adventure series starring Darren McGavin. Reynolds and McGavin did not get along, however. Commenting afterwards, Burt said, "I will say this about McGavin. He is going to be a very disappointed man on the first Easter after his death. I was a green kid insofar as film was concerned. Instead of helping me, McGavin looked on me with contempt. He did everything but destroy me on camera; like we'd run through a scene a couple of times and just before the camera rolled, he'd say to me under his breath, 'You're not going to play it *that* way, are you?' And what little confidence I had would go right down the drain."

Long before Burt became the superstar he is today, shortly after he had begun to play the part of Quint Asper, the half-Indian blacksmith on "Gunsmoke," he gave one of those interviews that so many other actors on their way up have done. It was almost as fictional as the roles he played on television. It was also long before ethnicity was "in," and one of the first points made by the interviewer was that Burt was *not* part Indian.

The story went on to tell all about Burt's unhappy experience on the "Riverboat" series. It included his feelings about other actors he worked with, Jim Arness, Milburn Stone, and Ricardo Montalban. He said they were "guys who go out of their way to help you all they can." Referring to McGavin he said, "I'd like to work McGavin again, just once. I don't ask him to like me. I just want to make him respect me." It would be interesting to hear the reactions of both men to that statement today.

*A celebration of Burt's engagement to starlet Lori Nelson (left) during work on "Riverboat"*

When the first season of "Riverboat" was over, Burt left. He is candid about the circumstances today. He says, "I was in twenty-six segments of a serie called "Riverboat," where I got to fight with the Captain, Darren McGavin, mos the the times, then I got fired....Clint Eastwood and me got it the same day. The told Clint his Adam's apple was too big, and they told me I had no talent. It was big favor, though I didn't really think of it that way at the time."

Now, at the time for an actor to admit to getting fired was akin to confes sing that he was bald, wore elevator shoes, and had a sex life. To eve suggest such an admission sent agents scurrying for their tranquilize or liquor cabinets. They firmly believed that it was the kiss of death to a pe former's career.

The story was given to the press that Burt had wanted out, that he could n longer stand working in the series. "I wasn't doing anything and I wasn't learning anything, he reputedly said. "I had lines like 'Are the Indians going to attack us?' I was nothing but a dumdum Riverboat pilot. Revue [Productions] must have a whole auditorium packed with my closeups. None of them ever got on the air." Burt probably had been warned that failure to make such a comment would result in instant ostracism.

The story went on to tell with an air of deep sincerity that the producers tried to talk Burt out of quitting, but that he insisted he must leave, darkly threatening that he would "blow the damn riverboat up" if he wasn't let out of his contract. His agent, who had no intention of offending a production studio that would hire other clients, went along with the story and was quoted as reassuring them that he would indeed blow it up if he said so, and that they had better let him out of his contract—or else. Then came the part in which Burt was allegedly given a stern lecture about ingratitude, et cetera, et cetera. Probably the only valid part of the whole story was reflected in one line, in which Burt was quoted as having said: "Then I couldn't get a job at any major outfit. I didn't have a very good reputation."

Burt was frustrated and hostile. He hung around bars and had a tendency to drink too much. He also fell into the habit of picking fights with the first character to so much as look at him cross-eyed. He recalled, "I'd drive down to the skid row section, walk into a bar, wait for the inevitable crack, belt the guy in the teeth, and go home feeling much better." He did whatever he could to work, observing, "I did every lousy syndicated show they were making, I did some things like "Pony Express," the kind of shows they shoot with a Kodak and a flashlight. Those were depressing years, but that's where I finally learned how to act."

When he could not find acting jobs, he worked as a stunt man. As Burt himself put it, "I crashed cars and fell out of buildings until I eventually landed a regular part on "Gunsmoke." I guess I could have stayed on that show for years and made very good money, but I didn't want to limit myself to halfbreed roles for the rest of my life."

Except for a brief return to New York for a Broadway show in October 1961, Burt stuck it out in Hollywood. On Broadway he played Skip, a crude, brutish sailor in a play *Look: We've Come Through*. Decent reviews notwithstanding, the show folded after 5 performances, and Burt flew back to the West Coast.

Before Burt settled down into a 2½-year stint on "Gunsmoke," from 1962 until 1965, he was virtually type-cast as either a heavy or an Indian on a number of shows, all of which have faded into oblivion. He also played in two feature films. *Angel Baby*, in 1961, starred George Hamilton, Mercedes McCambridge, Salome Jens, and Joan Blondell. *Armored Command*, also in 1961, starred Howard Keel, Tina Louise, and Earl Holliman.

It was in his role as Quint Asper, the blacksmith on "Gunsmoke," that the public first began to recognize and appreciate Burt Reynolds. He described Quint as "a guy who loves physical contact, has no prejudices, is completely independent, takes people at face value, and would just as soon fight as eat." Regarding his role in "Gunsmoke" now, Burt observes, "If you don't remember me, I don't blame you. I was the halfbreed blacksmith who got to get Marshall Dillon his horse once in every great while."

**P**erhaps the part was no great challenge; nevertheless, it was during this series that Burt began getting the kind of professional recognition that is so vital to the career of an actor. During his first season on "Gunsmoke," producer Norman Macdonnell spotted Burt's potential, and said, "I have the feeling that if he ever got the bit in his teeth, he'd run away with it. He's not afraid of man, beast, or God. Yet he's really made an effort to fit in with us. It's not easy for a newcomer to break into a cast that's been working together like a family all these years. I think he's a good actor. Innately, he's a leading man, which creates something of a problem for us. We can't use him as such. But we get so many letters saying, 'Enjoyed the show last night with Matt, Kitty, Doc, and the blacksmith.' That's damning him with faint praise, in a way, yet, it means the character has been established. I think next season he'll begin to make a real impact." Macdonnell's comments were made before the end of Burt's first season on the show.

Burt recognized how important praise was to an actor, and what a dangerous enemy indifference could be. He commented, both on himself and on the part he was playing in the series, "I don't care how good or bad I am so long as I am not dull."

Burt Reynolds' next series, "Hawk," was a big step forward in more ways than one. First of all it was his own series. He was the leading man. Secondly it was a stereotype-breaker. The character he played was another Indian, but this time he was a New York detective. He said that his idea of the character he played was "a man who didn't talk gibberish or get plastered," but he was alone in his opinion. He recalled "If everybody else had had their way, I'd have been running around in moccasins and feathers with knives up my sleeves." Whatever the problems were, the rewards were greater. Looking back, he said, " 'Hawk' was one of the happiest years of my life in this business. For the first time, I didn't feel like a chess pawn. I helped direct, cast, and write scripts."

**J**ournalist Seli Groves, a former fan magazine editor and veteran star-watcher, recalled doing an interview with Burt Reynolds while he was filming "Hawk" in New York in 1966. She said, "One of the reasons Burt came to New York to do "Hawk" was that he had a great affection for the city. It had been very good to him when he was starting out in show business. He told me how the people he had met in New York encouraged him and gave him the first real hope that he would succeed. And of course, his principal reason for doing "Hawk" was that it was his first leading role. Before that he was really known only as a supporting actor, as in "Gunsmoke.""

"He told me that he felt the American Indian image in films and television hadn't been accurately represented. He talked about his own Indian ancestors, about his grandmother. She was a Seminole, I believe. He felt that Indians were either portrayed as savages or pitiable conquered characters. On the other hand, as Hawk, a New York police detective, the imagery was full of the most positive elements he could think of. Virility, intelligence, derring-do. The fact that he was a New York City detective was indicative of how much he appreciated New York as a city. He said he considered it in a sense, a tribute to New York.

*scene from "Gunsmoke", 1963*

"Burt impressed me as a very warm man and one with an amazing instinct for publicity, among other things. Later, when I was based in California myself, I met a number of other reporters, editors, publicists — people who were very close to Burt, and they all said very positive things about him, that he was genuinely eager to help people.

"I remember once I got a call from someone working with him who had learned that I knew a great deal about American Indians. It seems that a query had come in to Burt from a Sunday supplement somewhere about Indians. It was going to be published in a question-and-answer column, and Burt was so anxious that the story be done accurately, when he found out that compared to himself I was an expert, he had the query directed to me. I did all the additional research, based on what I already knew, and Burt used it. He was very appreciative and a little nonplussed because he hadn't known the answers, so he made up his mind to learn them, so he could answer any questions that came up next time."

Those who remember the "Hawk" series will probably recall that it was considerably better than much of its competition on the other networks. It was sheer bad luck that "Hawk" was competing with feature films already underway elsewhere. The programming executives at ABC canceled the show, paying no attention to its intrinsic merits, but going strictly according to the ratings game. They canceled "Hawk" mid-season, despite angry protests from fans.

Writing in the *New York World Telegram* on January 4, 1967, Al Salerno reported, "Letters by the hundreds, including one with 250 signatures, have poured into this newspaper. It is known that the network also received substantial protest mail....The letter-writers raged against the network holding on to so much of what it considers pap while cutting off a strong, adult drama with a forceful central character well-acted by Burt Reynolds."

For the next 3 years, Burt played in a number of eminently forgettable B pictures he described as the type that "they show in airplanes and prisons because nobody can leave." He also referred to them as "classics of what *not* to make if you want to make a good movie." Then he was offered his next series, "Dan August," another cop show. When producer Quinn Martin first approached Burt with the part he said, "No, I've had it with cop parts." But then, he recalled, [Martin] "offered me some money, and I still said I don't want to play another cop, and then he made a *ridiculous* offer and I said, 'Gee, I always wanted to play a cop,' and I sold out."

In "Dan August," Burt played a detective in a small, unnamed city on the West Coast. The series ran on ABC in 1970–1971 and reran on CBS in the summer of 1973, after which it was canceled for good. When interviewed by Betty White for the *Saturday Evening Post* in 1978, Burt looked back at his three series experiences and, grinning philosophically, told her, "I'm probably the only actor who has ever been canceled on all three networks."

*With director Paul Bogart during production of "Hawk" (pages 30-31); in "Dan August" (pages 32-33); with unidentified actress in* Impasse, 1969 *(left)*

# F O U R

# ON THE
# BRINK
# OF
# CELEBRITY

Even though he had enjoyed a fairly public career by 1966, and was the star of "Hawk" at the time, Burt Reynolds' name was yet to become a household word. Probably there were scores of fans who would have recognized his face but would not have known his name; conversely, there were probably those who knew his name but did not necessarily recall his face. It was one of the peculiarities of early television that had not yet completely faded away.

One evening that autumn, after the Dallas Cowboys had played the New York Giants in the last game of the season, Burt went with his friend, Don Meredith, and a group of other Dallas Cowboys to a very posh cocktail party in a luxury apartment located on New York's exclusive Sutton Place.

Writing about the events of the evening in *Sports Illustrated* of May 30, 1974, journalist Edwin Shrake described the locale of the party as "a New York apartment that looked kind of like the King Farouk suite at a four-star hotel, full of jewels, furs, carpets, paintings, dressy women and silver ice buckets full of foil bottlenecks sticking out...," a place where "some of the rooms had steps in them and the little glass tables behind the rubber plants were loaded with ornaments no Chinese emperor will ever see again."

As Burt, Don Meredith, and the other Cowboys arrived and gathered in the foyer to hand their coats to a maid, word spread that the football team had arrived. As Shrake tells it, "A tall woman who had more ice on her fingers than she did in her drink approached Meredith and smiled.

"'You must be Lee Roy Jordan,' the woman said.

"'Yes ma'am, I am,' said Meredith. 'I love to hit people and knock 'em down. I sock 'em good. I really do. I purely love it.'

"'Which one is Don Meredith?' the woman said.

"'Bless your heart, he's this cute rascal right behind me,' said Meredith. 'You ought to get to know him a lot better. There's nothing but pearls comes out of his mouth.'

"The woman bore in on Reynolds and pressed him toward the wall, telling him that he looked like a tremendously physical person, not quite as big as she had expected, maybe, but terribly physical nevertheless, and it was a thrilling experience for her to meet a famous quarterback.

"'It was incredible to me,' Reynolds remembers. 'Almost nobody at that party knew who I was, but this woman heard me identified as Don Meredith, and so here she came with all this cleavage and diamonds. I had a lot of fun holding court, pretending to be Meredith, talking about Freudian interpretations of football, anything else I could have fun with, and people gathered around, took it all in. I thought: *So this is what it's like.*'"

**B**urt had a great deal to think about at this particular juncture of his life: divorce, for one thing. Three years earlier he had married Judy Carne, the British-born actress who later became "Laugh-In's" sock-it-to-me girl. At the time they met, he was still a relative newcomer and she was the star of an extremely popular series called "Love on a Rooftop." Their marriage was a glittering media event. Writing about Judy Carne in *Redbook*, Claire Safran described her as quite different from all the girls who had attracted Burt in the past, "more pixyish than pretty, with a slender, almost boyish body...a free spirit, the first flower child, a Peter Pan." For the year they were living together he found those qualities in her "terribly exciting." But for the rest of their 3-year marriage, it was, Claire wrote, "more than he could handle."

"Sometimes," Burt confided to her, "the things that attract you in the first place are the things that drive you crazy in marriage. But if you come from the kind of background I do, you think about settling down and having babies. So I said, 'Wait a minute. We have to change. I've been watching "Father Knows Best" and we're not doing this right.' But that was ridiculous. Why should she change? That's what I fell in love with. The divorce was my fault, my loss. She's a terrific person."

By the time that Burt had been interviewed for *Redbook*, the wounds had healed. It was 1974. But when Seli Groves met with him in 1966 they were still raw and fresh. It was while he was still working on "Hawk." The divorce hadn't come through yet. Seli asked him about the marriage and recalls, "He wouldn't talk about it. He believed that a marriage was a private affair between two people, and what went wrong was their business and no one else's. He said he had hoped the marriage would succeed, but that it hadn't."

Commenting on the marriage, Betty White observed, "Reynolds was not an easy person to live with either. He had a 'rotten temper' and a proclivity for settling disputes with his fists. It was Judy who helped him see that slugging his way through life was counterproductive. 'God, you're boring,' she said after one wild altercation."

In 1968 or thereabouts, Seli Groves sought out Judy Carne and interviewed her at the Smokehouse in Burbank, California. Recalling the interview she told

*The wedding of Burt and Judy Carne*

me, "After we established a very nice rapport, she finally talked about Burt, because at first she hadn't wanted to. She said that the major problem in their marriage was political. He was right wing and she was left wing. Even that could have been worked out, she thought, but he was rigid in his views, and never even wanted to argue a point out in politics, or even their careers. He had a goal and he intended to stick to it. When we spoke she said that she still loved him very much and would liked to have heard from him. She said she hoped that when my interview was printed it would lead him to call her. She said she still hoped for a reconciliation, but was realistic enough to realize that Burt rarely went back; however, she felt that they could be friendlier than they were then."

Not long afterwards they did succeed in maintaining a friendly contact, and, as Burt told Claire Safran in 1974, "We're still terribly attracted to each other. We had something special together.... But why would I want to rekindle anything temporarily? I'm very happy right now. I don't want to complicate my life or hers. We've hurt each other enough."

In 1966, however, when the divorce was final, Burt was anything but happy. He was the first member of his family ever to have undergone a divorce, and to him it symbolized failure on a grand scale. He was temporarily devastated. He thought about how hurt and angry his father had been when he dropped out of Florida State College. The only thing he could think of now was failure — football, two TV series, and now, in marriage.

In a fit of depression he picked up the phone, called his mother, and said, "Tell Dad he was right about me. Tell him I'm a quitter." Before anyone could speak, Burt's father, who had picked up the extension phone, said, "Come on home. I'll tell you about all the things I've quit in my life."

Recalling the incident with emotion, Burt says, "My father and I would still be strangers if he hadn't said that to me. Thank God he did. I caught the first plane home....In the house he offered me a drink. My father and I took a bottle of cognac outside and talked all night long. We got smashed together and I hugged him and he hugged me. He started talking about the mistakes he'd made. I'd never *known* him to make a mistake. Suddenly he was a totally different man. I cried. And he got tears in his eyes. Now my dad and I are embarrassing—running around and grabbing each other in airports. We always hug and kiss each other."

# F I V E

# MR. MACHO, THE TALK SHOWS, AND THAT CENTERFOLD

So there he was. No wife, no television series, no starring movie roles. He had nothing but a fair track record, a lot of largely unrecognized talent, and something very dangerous for an actor anxious to make the big time: an image that locked him into super macho, 2-dimensional roles. He said, "They thought of me as a brutish Marlon Brando type, being cast in that kind of role because Brando had priced himself out of that kind of thing and was getting old."

But even actors have to pay the grocer, the landlord and the utility companies. They also know that if they don't maintain the right kind of high profile and keep the public constantly aware of their presence, the next thing they know they will be deader than last year's turkeys after Thanksgiving. So as he had done in the early sixties, Burt accepted every part that came along.

There were, however, some discerning critics who recognized the fact that beneath all of this there lurked a potential star. He was a good actor in the wrong vehicles. In an interview he gave to Roberta Brandes Gratz for the *New York Post* on October 9, 1969, he said, "It's amazing that they see it and the people with the money don't. Somebody is going to have to take a chance on me." He had not, as yet, learned how to take chances on himself.

What annoyed Burt, as he told Bob Lardine for an interview in the New York *Daily News* magazine, "You'd be surprised how narrow-minded the people with the big money and the top scripts can be. When a terrific story comes along they'll say, 'Reynolds isn't right for it. He can only play rednecks and rough humor.' And when a David Niven comedy pops up they ignore me and give it to George Segal who's already appeared in four pictures that I would've loved to have done: *Blume in Love, Where's Poppa?, The Owl and the Pussycat*, and *A Touch of Class*. The producers also don't think I'm refined enough to do Robert Redford pictures. I guess it's because he's kind of pretty and hails from the Yale-Harvard school of acting.

"I would have given anything to be in *All the President's Men*. Even if it hadn't been Redford's property I wouldn't have come close to nailing down a lead role. The only part I might have gotten was playing one of the Cubans — 'Hey! You there! Get up off the wall or I'll blow your head off!'"

Burt went on to say, "Don't you think I would have jumped at the opportunity to play Jack Nicholson's role in *One Flew Over the Cuckoo's Nest*? For a while, I thought I was going to get it, too. I was that close to nailing down the picture. I think it would have been a major turning point for me. It would have meant something with critics like John Simon and Pauline Kael. People keep saying to me, 'Why don't you do a picture like *Butch Cassidy and the Sundance Kid*?' The reason I don't is that no one offers them to me. All I get are forty-five different versions of *White Lightning* or thirty-five stories like *Fuzz*. I don't think I'm stupid. I read all the material offered me, and do the best stuff from it."

What Burt finally realized was that he was going to have to take his career into his own hands and do something about it. He was going to have to take chances. As he put it, "I was the tight, constipated, actor. I just stood there with my number three virile look and never took chances."

The time for taking chances hadn't quite arrived, but it was very much on the horizon. He was about to become a talk show personality. The first major show to have Burt on as a guest was Merv Griffin. Burt and Merv hit it off from the

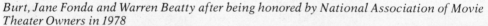

*Burt, Jane Fonda and Warren Beatty after being honored by National Association of Movie Theater Owners in 1978*

44

start. It was there that Burt gained confidence as a personality, as opposed to an actor working with a script and a director in a studio. His experience in the theatre stood him in very good stead. Nevertheless, there is quite a difference between performing in a play and being thrown to the wolves as a talk show guest. There are so many factors with which to contend. There is the matter of the studio audience, the host, the technicians. There are distractions on a talk show that can drive the novice guest into a state of cardiac arrest. Perhaps it looks to the viewer like a private conversation made public. It is anything but that, however. Being a shrewd observer of things as they are, Burt saw from the beginning what went into the creation of an ideal talk show personality. He made up his mind then and there that he would either do it right or not at all.

He appeared on the Merv Griffin show 11 times before he even considered doing anyone else's show. "By the eleventh time," Burt said, "I wanted to try hosting one. I asked Merv's people and they said I wasn't ready yet. The next time Johnny Carson asked me to be on his show, I said, 'yes,' and by the second commercial, he leaned over to me and asked me if I wanted to host his show. I immediately said that I'd love to."

It was via the talk show route that a whole new image of Burt Reynolds emerged and took shape before the public eye. His awareness, his wit, his ability to think on his feet, and his distinctive sense of humor turned the tide. Although he readily admits that Merv Griffin was the first host to give him a break, he says unequivocally, "I must give the Carson show credit for turning the people of the industry around and getting the variety show guest spots and *good* film parts."

**B**urt had been in New York to host the Carson show. He says, "I was having a good time. By that time I knew a lot of warm and witty people, the so-called 'fun crowd,' and I always held my own with them....When I came back to Hollywood, director John Boorman called me into his office to talk about being in *Deliverance*. I said, 'What in the world have you seen on film that would make you want me to be in this movie?' and he said, 'I saw you on the "Tonight" show.' I said, 'This is not a funny movie. What did you see that made you want me?' He said he saw a man in control. There were six people on the panel and, he said, 'You were maneuvering them all. You were in control of them and that's what I want in this character. Can you do a southern accent?'"

Burt had spent 12 years getting rid of his southern accent. He told the English director where he came from, grinned, and said, "Give me five minutes and I'll get it back for you." Boorman knew exactly what he wanted from Burt and was certain he could get the performance from him that he anticipated would be forthcoming. Lewis Medlock, the character Burt played in *Deliverance*, was a man both powerful and vulnerable. He was the leader of 3 businessmen from Atlanta who go off for a weekend canoe trip, and who find themselves forced into a situation that tests them and radically changes their lives.

A seething drama, *Deliverance* was as turbulent as the river rapids on which much of the action occurred. A multifaceted suspense story that never lets up, it was many things to many people. Some thought of it merely as a story about four men on a canoe trip who encounter tragedy. Others regarded it as a cinematic essay on rape — man's rape of man, against a background of man's

45

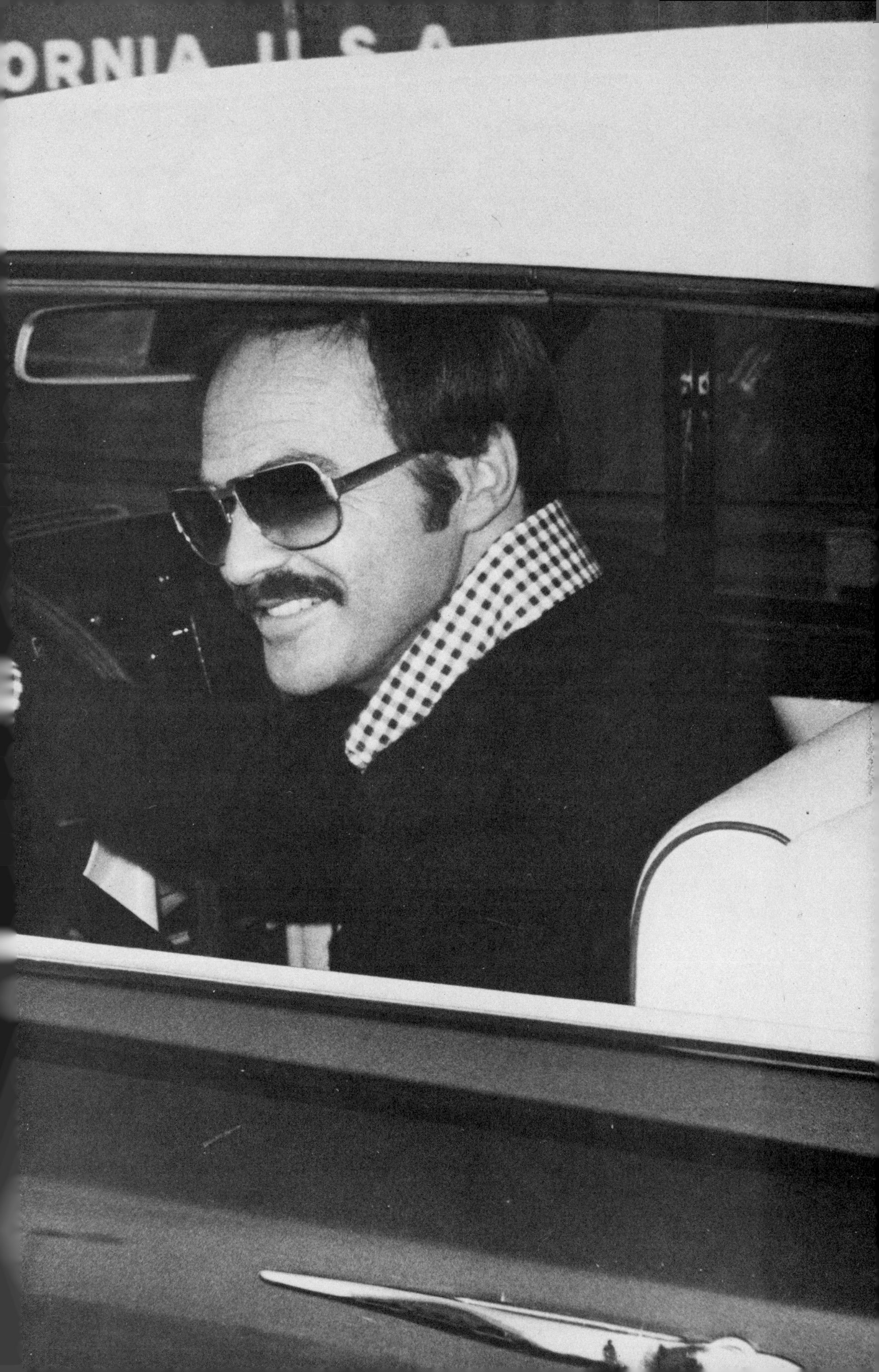
ORNIA U S A

*A scene from* Deliverance

rape of his own environment. *Deliverance* was a masterful shocker with a searing impact, and Burt Reynolds was robust and bursting with energy. *Time* observed, "The movie was Reynolds' own deliverance. Overnight he became the Frog Prince of Hollywood."

When Burt started working on *Deliverance*, he met Jon Voight for the first time, and the two of them hit it off at once. Not realizing the extent of his own acting ability, Burt said, "I was afraid Jon Voight would blow me off the screen. The director, John Boorman, kept telling me how good I was, but I didn't believe it. Then one night Voight, a guy I'd become good friends with, asked me how I was going to handle things after the picture was released. He said *Deliverance* was going to do for me what *Midnight Cowboy* did for him. I told Jon I'd been hearing that bull for years, I didn't need to hear it from him. He said no, he could smell it, it was true. So I started believing it and it happened."

If the year 1972 saw Burt Reynolds catapulted to stardom for his role in *Deliverance*, it is also memorable for something else that had a great deal to do with his escalating popularity; it was the year that Burt agreed to pose for that notorious *Cosmopolitan* nude centerfold. "I felt it would be a kick," he said. "It was all a joke. I did it to satirize *Playboy* and all those other centerfolds."

Elaborating on why he did it Burt added, "I felt I had the sense of humor to bring it off after the magazine came out. I was fully prepared to get in an elevator with a bunch of guys and either have to be funny or fight my way out. But men seem to recognize the humor in it faster than women. Of course there are always guys who love to show off by calling you a movie star faggot, but most guys just laugh and kid me about it."

Once the word was out that Burt was going to do a nude for *Cosmopolitan*, the general prognosis was that it would make him a laughing stock. But instead of that happening, what Burt himself intended came to pass. All over the country women picked up copies of *Cosmopolitan*, some as a gag, some to kid their husbands or lovers, and still others for the same reason that men buy similar photographs of undraped women.

As Seli Groves wrote in "Burt Reynolds: The Man Behind the 'Good Old Boy,'" "Initially, when he posed for that spread by top photographer Francesco Scavullo, he knew that he was risking his career if the photo that ran resulted in a backlash of resentment, indignation, ire, and other assorted negative reactions. But he also knew that nothing got one's name into the papers and, thus, into the consciousness of both fan and filmmakers as did some honest to goodness (or honest to naughtiness!) exposure!

"Well, the photo did run and the magazine sold out every single issue it had printed! The poster people, too, toted up terrific profits running those big broad blowups of Burt in all his masculine magnificence! (Or very nearly all!) Fans cried for more of these fetching poses. But there would be no more. Not that this was the only pic the talented Scavullo had caught in his lenses that fateful day Burt posed for him. Hardly. It's said that several contact sheets were produced at that sitting meaning that there could be at least a dozen or so sharply in-focus shots of Burt looking like a cigar-smoking, hairy-chested kewpie doll. But Scavullo did not own the photos; Burt did. Clever Burt Reynolds made sure of

*Escorting Sally Fields*

that. And he also made sure that no other photos from that set would run in a public medium. Why? Because he had made his point. He had startled people out of their lethargy and made himself a permanent imprint on their imaginations. Any more such 'revealing' photos would simply dilute the results."

The day finally arrived that the highly touted issue of *Cosmopolitan* hit the stands. Heated debates were going on all over the country as to whether the appearance of the celebrated shot would advance Burt's career or knock it back to square one. Particularly apprehensive were the executives of Warner Brothers, who were concerned that a naked Burt Reynolds would detract from the serious image of *Deliverance*, which they were hoping would prove to be a blockbuster.

While Helen Gurley Brown sat in her office on West 57th Street in Manhattan, rubbing her hands together and chortling with anticipation, Burt was doing some serious thinking about the same subject, but along different lines. It just so happened that on publication day he had been booked as guest host of the "Tonight" show. No fool he, Burt had planned it well in advance, referring to it afterwards as a calculated move. Describing his game plan he told interviewer Edwin Shrake of *Sports Illustrated*, "For the opening monologue I told the writers to think of me as Don Rickles doing a routine on Burt Reynolds, and to use every terrible, rotten joke on me they could think of. By the time I'd finished that monologue there was nothing left for people to say, I'd said it all. And I've still got my savers—one-liners that I use. Like maybe I get on a plane and a guy whistles at me, and I say, 'Thanks, the flowers were beautiful.' I was in a restaurant one night, and the violinist looked down at me and said, 'You wouldn't be anything if it hadn't been for that magazine picture.' So I told him he ought to pose for one and then he could be playing at Carnegie Hall."

Actually, when Burt first saw the picture as it was published, he wasn't that happy about it. As he said, "It looked like I'd been studying humility with Gene Barry. Apparently the people at *Cosmo* took this thing more seriously than I did." He admitted that he expected to be the butt of jokes. He said he was fully prepared to be whistled at by women. when he got on airplanes, adding with a grin, "But that's okay, I happen to like women."

*Burt and Sally Fields in* Smokey and the Bandit

# S I X

# THE WOMEN IN HIS LIFE

Despite the fact that he always had an eye for the ladies—his macho image notwithstanding—Burt Reynolds never made any secret of the fact that he didn't especially care for his reputation as a sex symbol. "The only way to handle it," he said, "is to laugh with it. Go with it. Have fun with it. If you take it seriously it can be as damaging to a man as it has been to some women. Like Marilyn Monroe.... Sex symbols don't last very long."

Though he has always made it a point to date and be seen with the most glamorous women in the headlines, he has ever been one to go tearing off on a series of wild, one-night stands. Maybe the myth was great for the deliberately crafted image of a "flip, cocky bastard" that gave him the clout to become a movie star, but it did not and does not fit the man. When he talked to Joe Baltake for *Us* he said, "I'm just no good with women who are swingers. I don't like what they do or what they represent. My idea of a good time with a woman is to hole up for three days and watch old movies, make pizza, be silly, act like children and get the giggles."

A man who knows who he is and where he is going, Burt Reynolds has never had qualms about taking advantage of his reputation. He has a philosophical attitude toward life and the older he gets the more adept he becomes at making every situation work for him without hurting anyone else. Quite an accomplishment. So what if he is reputed to be one of the smoothest woman-chasers in the business? As he said to Bob Lardine, "I know people figure I won't ever marry again because I'm such a swinger. But the reason I haven't married is that I'm really a big square. I want a marriage like the ones all my friends enjoy. All my pals like Mel Brooks and Dom DeLuise are happily married and that's why I like to be around them and their wives. It's very difficult finding the right girl when you're continually working."

Recognizing the value of publicity, he observes, "No—it doesn't bother me to read that I'm out with a different woman every night. Sometimes seeing my name in print with a gal actually gives me an excuse to meet her. I don't even know most of the women I'm supposed to be in love with."

Burt also has a superb talent for endearing himself to his female fans, whether they are serious film buffs, straight admirers, or screaming groupies. He knows perfectly well that without them he would not be a star. He appreciates them and he takes as much care of them as he can without compromising anyone. He said, "One of the important things I've learned is not to run from them. The minute you do they'll start chasing you.... You might as well have fun with all the attention because you never know when it's going to end."

Unlike some stars who have upon occasion succeeded in being downright rude when confronted by wild, inconsiderate mobs of fans, Burt is extremely tolerant. He never loses his cool. No matter how heavy the going gets he manages to treat the situation lightly, thereby endearing himself even more to the fans. He says, "Sure, girls come knocking on my hotel door in the middle of the night, but that's no problem. I just go out and talk to them, and usually that's all they want." Then, after dealing with the sex symbol business with absolute seriousness, he practices what he preaches by making fun of it, saying, "The other night I nearly killed myself trying to live up to a typographical error. It's amazing how much a three looks like an eight."

The legend of Burt Reynolds as a womanizer gained considerable momentum in the late sixties after his divorce from Judy Carne. He was seen or linked with

*Burt with Catherine Deneuve in* Hustle

some of the most glamorous women in filmdom. There was actress Lori Nelson, the gorgeous Greta Baldwin, and the exotic Miko Myania. After the movie, *Skulduggery*, Burt made romantic headlines with actress Susan Clark, and during the filming of *Hustle*, rumors flew like sparks about Burt and Catherine Deneuve. As time passed the list grew longer and more impressive. It came to include such glamour queens as Candice Bergen, Sarah Miles, Liza Minnelli, and Farrah Fawcett-Majors. Tennis star Chris Evert also managed to have her name linked to Burt's once.

When he dated Farrah Fawcett she was just another curvy blonde starlet with an impressive inventory of physical attributes. Much later on, after she had become all the rage, Burt confessed that he had given serious consideration to marrying her at one time. Looking back he said, "I waited too long and a friend of mine named Lee Majors won her as his wife." Burt insisted that had he moved faster, today she probably would be known as Farrah Fawcett-Reynolds.

There is no doubt that Burt's most widely publicized romance was with Dinah Shore. Neither of them made any bones about their love affair. It was honest, open, and totally lacking in negative aspects. Neither of them cared about the age difference between them. There was a tremendous amount of give and take. As Seli Groves observed, "Their love affair was a great shot in the emotional arm, from its metaphor, for older women. If Dinah could get a man like that in her life, why couldn't anyone else? One reporter with a wire service, who was very close to Burt told me that whatever the romantic implications of the Burt-Dinah relationship might have been — an actual go-to-bed situation — there was genuine affection between the two, and a genuine need for friendship that each could supply to the other...Burt got a great deal of publicity during the time he and Dinah were together, and he was on her show several times. In fact that was how they met, on her show. Another interesting point was that Dinah's children were very fond of Burt Reynolds. And it worked both ways. Dinah's son, in particular, looked at Burt not only as a friend, but as a male idol, very much in the model of George Montgomery."

A fascinating aspect of the Burt–Dinah affair was its wholesomeness, and the willingness on both of their parts to discuss it with dignity. Talking about it to Claire Safran, Burt was very candid when he agreed with Claire that they were a very mismatched couple on the surface. He said, "I should be dating Angel Tompkins and Dinah should be going with Henry Kissinger....We met when I was filming *Deliverance*. She wanted to visit me on location but I said 'No.' I was worried about her image. I didn't know how terribly capable she was about handling anything. She's deceptive that way." He went on to say, "I made a pact with her in the very beginning, we would just make the best of it as long as it lasted. Be honest with each other for as long as it lasted. If that was forever, terrific. If not, we didn't want to hurt each other."

Burt made it plain that marriage was not in the offing as far as he and Dinah were concerned. Both recognized that it was most likely something that would not work. And indeed, it did finally come to an end after 5 years, rather abruptly it seemed to the public. But it ended neither with a bang nor a whimper. There were no histrionics, no lamentations, no gnashing of teeth or tearing of hair.

*Burt and Dinah Shore*

Most important, there were no verbal barrages of enmity. No enmity at all. On the contrary, they remained, and still remain, very close friends. Talking about it in retrospect Burt said, "People castigated Dinah for taking up with a man 19 years her junior; then they turned around and pilloried me for 'walking out on her.' Dinah is still my best friend. We talk often and she is still very special to me." He added as an afterthought, "If I have any class at all, it's due to Dinah."

Burt also referred to Dinah as "the happiest person I know…and the classiest. There was no way I couldn't be the heavy when we agreed to be just friends. She could have cut me up and run me over with a car and the papers would say, 'Burt jilts Dinah.'" As it was the press had no reason to be caustic toward either of them. Both of them happened to be very well liked and have never given the press cause to treat them with anything but respect.

There is little doubt that one of the reasons Burt will always have a warm place in his heart for Dinah Shore has to do with how she stood by him during one of the most traumatic experiences in his career. It was 1973. Burt was

playing the lead in *The Man Who Loved Cat Dancing*, opposite Sarah Miles. There were the usual unfounded innuendoes about Burt and Sarah. They liked one another. They worked well together and were seen in public together doing such scandalous things as having dinner. But beyond that there was absolutely nothing between them.

While they were on location in Gila Bend, Arizona, Sarah's business manager/lover, David Whiting, who was clearly not in possession of all his faculties, became jealous one night. She had paid a visit on Burt in his room. Afterwards harsh words erupted between the pair and Whiting began to beat Ms. Miles. Hurt and frightened, she twisted out of his grasp and cried out to Burt for help. By the time he responded to her calls and came to her aid Whiting had left. Some time afterward Whiting was found dead.

Rumors began flying like sawdust around a buzz saw. Questions loaded with innuendo were fired off accusingly. How did Whiting happen to have a gash on his head? The autopsy revealed that Whiting had died from an overdose of

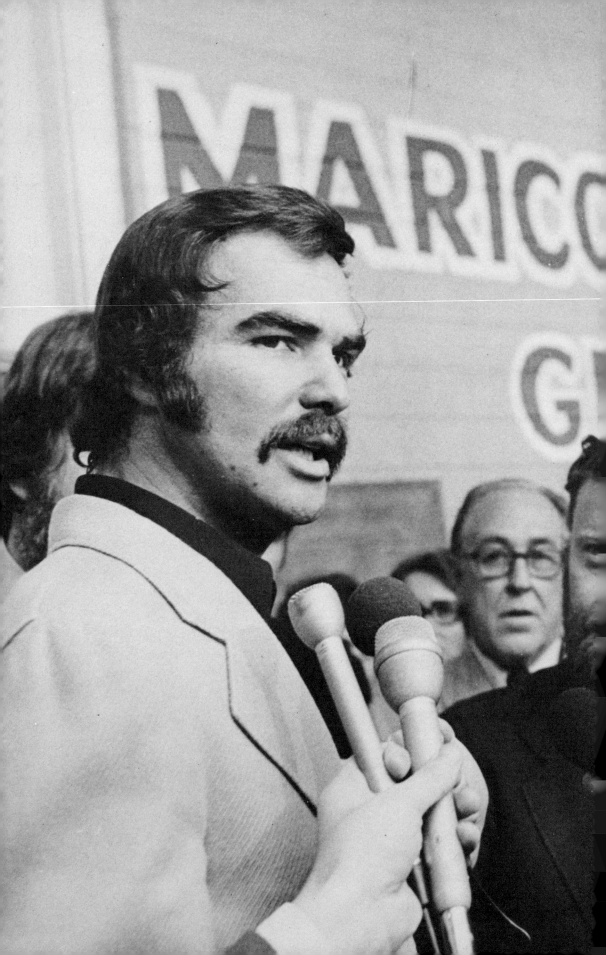

methaqualone. Nevertheless, most of the stories that found their way onto the front pages were noticeably lacking in statements from Burt Reynolds or Sarah Miles. When he discussed the matter with Claire Safran there was an understandable note of annoyance in his voice. "They left all those gaps in the stories. When you do that, lots of people fill in the gaps with ugly thoughts.... Yes," he admitted. "Sarah was in my room when I was getting a massage. Massage didn't used to be a dirty word. No, I didn't want Sarah there. I asked her to leave but she wouldn't."

He distinctly recalled her cries for help after returning to her own quarters, and he said, "If I had found Whiting beating Sarah up, then, being the male chauvinist pig that I am, I'd have fought with him. But he wouldn't have had that so-called gash, which was just a quarter-inch cut, probably the result of a fall. If I'd seen him, he'd probably be alive today. He'd have been too battered to get up and take those pills. I know the penalty for perjury," Burt continued. "I said on my oath that I did not see, touch or physically harm David Whiting that night. I would have been glad to say under oath that I did not have an affair with Sarah Miles, but nobody asked."

The aftermath of this nasty business left some very unpleasant scars on Burt. He was extremely disappointed with a number of people whom he had regarded as friends, but who didn't come forward when he needed them the most. He was also extremely resentful at sugestions by certain reporters that he might welcome the publicity he got from the matter. "What?" he exclaimed. "A man died! I found him! I will always see him lying there. Emotionally and physically, I just collapsed. I found out that it doesn't matter what shape your body is in; you can be destroyed from within."

But, as Burt was quick to point out, it was Dinah Shore who helped him the most at that time to keep his act together. "After Gila Bend she told reporters that it was only natural for Sarah to call on me for help. 'If I were in trouble,' she said, 'I'd call on Burt.' She never doubted, never questioned. That's class. I'd be happy if I had half of Dinah's class."

The number-one woman in Burt Reynolds life today, Sally Field, has been associated with him both professionally and personally. "One of the high points in his relationship with Sally Field," says Seli Groves, "is the fact that she provides him with a family situation as well as a male-female situation. She comes with her children and he likes that. They seem to be a close couple. They allow people to think of them as one day marrying, although it is doubtful that they need marriage at this point."

Burt has been very cautious about marriage since the failure of his first one, but it would seem that he is coming closer to that point with Sally Field than he has with anyone else since Judy Carne. On more than one occasion he has expressed a definite desire to have children. He was and still is devoted to Dinah Shore's offspring, and he refers to himself as a "surrogate father" to Sally Field's sons, Peter, aged 9, and Eli, aged 6. He looked after them while their mother went to Cannes to accept an award for her performance in *Norma Rae*. One evening he arranged a slumber party for them and their friends. After that, he supervised such activities as private screenings, picnics, and ball games.

*(overleaf) Talking to the press following the inquest of the death of Sarah Miles' manager*

*n the set of* **The Man Who Loved Cat Dancing** *with Sarah Miles*

According to columnist Marilyn Beck, Burt and Sally are on the verge of marriage. She quoted him as saying, "We're both scared to death of marriage. After all, we've each failed at marriage before. And when it's reached a point where I've said, 'Okay, let's do it, I can handle it,' she says, 'No, let's wait, I'm afraid.' And when she's said, 'Okay, let's do it, I'm ready,' I've said, 'Wait, I'm afraid.' But I think all of that has finally worked itself out." Burt said that other than such minor hangups over the matter, the major hurdle to their getting married was that involving Sally's sons. He said, "I've had to make them see I wasn't just a guy who wanted to be their mother's husband—that I had no intention of taking her away from them. But I've been working hard at establishing a relationship with them — and it looks like there can be no more excuses for Sally and me."

Their own hectic careers keep them very busy. Although they spent some time together on the island of Bora Bora in Spring, 1979, from the moment they returned to California they barely had a chance to see one another. Talking about it, Burt said, "We do spend our weekends together, but during the week Sally's wanted to be with her boys. They're the most important things in the world to her — and that's the way it should be." Whether they get married or not would seem academic at this point, for, as Burt has said, they are always together, "even when we are apart. That's all that's important for now."

# SEVEN

# BURT REYNOLDS' PHILOSOPHY OF LIFE

Whenever a reporter asks a question
have an answer ready.

Just in case the press doesn't
have a question, always have one
to offer them.

Keep smiling. In that way no one will
know whether you're hiding pain,
planning a desperate act, or really
feeling happy.

Always smile in the presence of a
strange woman. Maybe you might not
know who she is. Some day
you might want to.

Whenever you're introduced to someone for the first time, always notice
some little thing about them. That
makes it much easier for you to remember his or her name. And there's
nothing like remembering a person's
name to endear you to them.

Make it a point to keep a bottle of
champagne and some good *paté de
foie gras* in the refrigerator at all
times. Nothing will impress a date
more when she goes into the kitchen
to get a glass of water and starts
snooping in the fridge to see how
you're faring in the culinary depart-
ment as a bachelor.

Never fail to remove the
champagne and the *paté* before the
IRS man pays you a visit.

Look your best whenever you go out.
If you don't meet someone later, at
least you'll like your reflection before
you take off. If you do meet someone
you'll pat yourself on the back for
having spruced up in advance.

If you don't feel like being chased by
the opposite sex, don't run away. Have
fun, play it by ear, and stay in control.

As an actor, don't refuse to read any script that comes your way. There's a lot of nothing around, but in the midst of it all there's liable to be a winner.

Watch out regarding possessions or they will start possessing you. Sometimes the things that you want the most are the things that become enormous burdens to you.

The only way to become a better actor is to act, but don't overdo it. Remember there's more to life than being an actor.

Never accept a role you don't like.

Never stop learning.

Steer clear of playing tennis with Chris Evert. She's too good (for me).

*On location making his debut as a director in* Gator, *1976*

# E I G H T

# BURT REYNOLDS ON HIS PICTURES

Up until the time he was in *Deliverance*, Burt took just about every role that came his way. He took very little time off and he made one picture after another. Few were memorable. *Deliverance* changed everything. It was said by critics and others that the film was his finest achievement as an actor. "Sure, it was my best," said Burt. "But it also was the best material handed to me. I can always tell if a movie is going to be good or bad while making it, and I had positive vibes about *Deliverance*. Now with *Lucky Lady*, that was another story. I was miserable making it and didn't get along with Stanley Donen, the director. I thought it was one of my best acting performances, but the picture was put together as though it were cut with an electric fan."

Although almost all of the pictures made by Burt before *Deliverance* were strictly B-action flicks, he did make one film that gave him an opportunity to take advantage of his innate sense of comedy. He did the Woody Allen picture, *Everything You Always Wanted to Know About Sex (But Were Afraid to Ask)*. In *Saga*, Robert A. Cutter wrote, "It was about this time that the Burt Reynolds macho man, with lots of put-on humor was born. Maybe Woody Allen had something to do with it, maybe not. Reynolds' stance as a sort of anti-establishment figure within the establishment already was set from the two TV series that weren't great hits at the time of their first release….. His role as a macho man with humor was cooking on all burners after *Everything You Always Wanted to Know* — while critics were bored, bored, bored with his comedies, the people who buy tickets made him a genuine star right up there with Wayne, Eastwood, Redford and Newman."

Even though Burt was now being taken seriously as an actor, he was not nominated for any awards. Actually there were a lot of surprised people when he was not nominated for an Oscar for *Deliverance*. But when he did *The Longest Yard* in 1974, he found himself in a blockbuster.

In the film Burt plays an ex-football pro who had been kicked out of the league for shaving points. After doing an Attila-the-Hun number on a bitchy girlfriend, he winds up doing time in the local state pen. To make matters worse, he finds himself locked up in an institution ruled by a warden, played by Eddie Albert, who is a warped gridiron freak. He has assembled a semi-professional football team from the ranks of the guards, and sees to it that they get plenty of practice. Next he orders Burt to organize a team of inmates to play the guards. But there is a catch. He is also ordered to throw the game just so that the cons won't get the wrong idea about who is running the show.

As you can well imagine, this resulted in one of the most bone-crunching football sequences ever to be seen in a feature film. The game in the picture takes up a full 40 minutes of its total running time, which was one-quarter of its total length. Shooting of the game alone took 5 weeks of filming on a 6-day-a-week shooting schedule. During that time there were some serious injuries.

Talking about it afterward Burt said, "We worked hard to make the game real. Nitschke [Ray Nitschke of the Green Bay Packers] might have worked a little too hard. He hit me a couple of shots that made me feel like I'd exploded. I tried not to let anybody know how much they hurt. We had some semi-pros from Savannah in the film who were out to knock my head off, but I was pretty well protected. They did get Kapp though. Joe Kapp [formerly of the Minnesota Vikings] invented the word *macho*. I wouldn't fight him with an axe. These guys wanted to go home and tell their wives and girlfriends they had crushed an NFL star, and they hit Kapp late and knocked him out of the film.

"A strange thing started happening. I'd look at the faces in the huddle, and this wasn't a movie anymore. It wasn't even a game, it was a battle. The convict team lived and slept together. And so did the guards. Behind the walls at a maximum security prison one has a tendency to walk a little closer to one's buddies—the *Deliverance* syndrome, I call it. All day long the black jerseys wouldn't speak to the white jerseys. Once I threw a pass and some guy gave me a cheap shot, and our whole bench emptied and ran out on the field to take up for me. Meredith had told me how it was when a team developed a sense of loyalty, and here it was happening to us.

"There are a few little things in the game on film that don't look right, and I wish they weren't in there, but it can't be helped. For example. When I call a play in the huddle I might say, 'Split Left on 2.' Well, 'Split Left on 2' is not a play, as some big black dude who sat behind me at that Houston preview kept pointing out. But if we showed me calling the whole play—like 32 XY East Tight End Hook, Wide Z Pattern, and all of that—we'd take up so much time we'd lose the whole audience. Some of the plays I called in the huddle were made up on the spot, like a tackle eligible pass I threw to Ernie Wheelwright. Occasionally I'd run with the ball when [director] Robert Aldrich wasn't expecting it. Aldrich

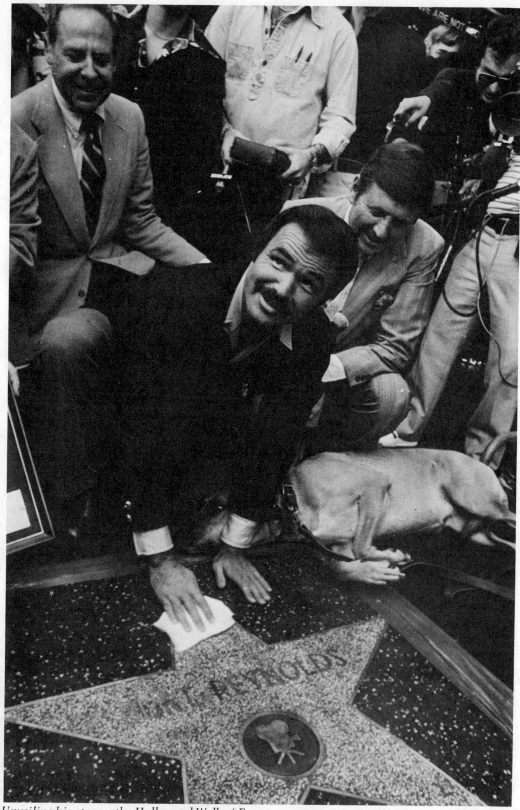

*Unveiling his star on the Hollywood Walk of Fame*

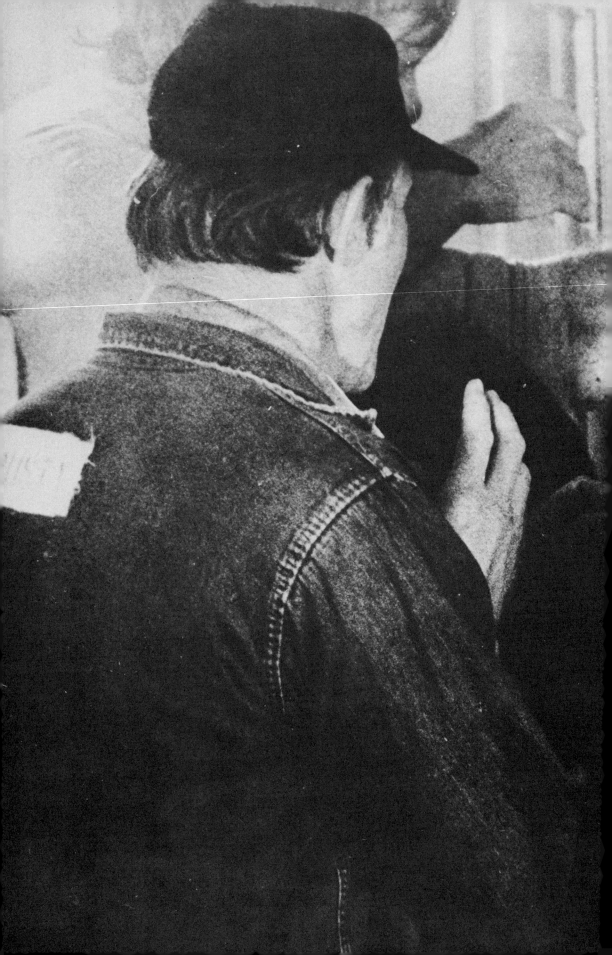

would give me hell, and I'd say I lost my head. But I knew it was terribly important for me to get my jock knocked off to make the film work."

One sequence where Burt finally scores a touchdown had to be shot several times. He took such a beating in it that director Aldrich was quoted later as saying that at the rate they were going, when they were done, Burt would wind up 3 inches shorter then when he had started.

In addition to football players, there were a number of seasoned stuntmen working on *The Longest Yard*. They all had the greatest respect for Burt because despite his star status, as far as they were concerned he was still very much one of them. Typical of this group was Frank Orsatti, who had worked with Burt many times over the years. Talking about Burt in an interview for *Sports Illustrated*, Orsatti said, "Burt likes guys he knows will go the limit. He always wants to be closely involved in the physical stuff, even if the studio won't let him actually take part. In *The Longest Yard*, I might have been killed if Glenn Wilder and Burt hadn't been standing by to safety for me."

Orsatti had been doing what is known among stuntmen as a fire gag, in which he was wrapped in tape, asbestos, rubber, clay and then set on fire. Unfortunately, more lighter fluid had been poured on him than was necessary and when he was ignited he nearly exploded. Burt and stuntman Glenn Wilder had to beat out the flames three times before he was fully extinguished.

Talking of his own past as a stuntman Burt said, "I'm always afraid somebody is going to tap me on the shoulder and say that from now on I'm going to get paid what I'm worth, which is about $3.50 an hour. I mean, nobody's worth what they pay me. That's part of the reason I try to get involved in my own stunts. It's not a question of macho. You get up in the morning, and somebody powders your face at 6 A.M., somebody else dresses you, somebody else moves you to a spot. By eleven, it's time to fall off a building and you feel you have to do it."

The macho comedies Burt made were also very important in establishing him not only as an actor worth watching but as a big star in the eyes of his public. The role he played in all of them was fashioned as much off the screen as on. He says, "I have worked very hard in the past few years to make it look as if I was being very natural, being myself, when I'm those macho, wisecracking guys. When I go on the "Tonight" show I have to say to myself in the green room, 'da da, da da, gotta get out there and be that guy!'" As a matter of fact it has been pointed out that Burt's dialogue in *The Longest Yard*, written by Keenan Wynn's son, Tracy Keenan Wynn, was supposedly based on a kind of speech pattern, rhythm, and delivery established by Burt while appearing on the "Tonight" show.

One of the other factors that made Burt's pictures so popular was his superb blending of humor and action. He says, "When I started in pictures, that makes me sound old I guess; well, when I started 20 years ago, there were two things, comedy and action—and the two rarely came together. Compare *White Lightning* with *Thunder Road*, which was a classic moonshine movie. Robert Mitchum never told any jokes, but in my picture, I was joking almost all of the time. I think it was a breakthrough, blending action and comedy in the way that it sells tickets and gets your point across.

"You notice, as soon as that picture made a lot of money, a lot of people started making that kind of picture, only they did it wrong. 'If he smashed up sixty cars and it made a lot of money, I'll smash up a hundred and make more.' But that had nothing to do with *Lightning*'s success. You've got to like the people in the picture for it to be successful, for it to be a major picture. You've got to have good scripts and actors."

He goes on to say "*Smokey* and *Longest Yard*, I think, were terrific films, better than most critics gave them credit for. When the gross is over 100 million dollars, a lot of people must like them. And in both of them, I was making a really conscious effort to have the time of my life in front of the camera. I think that's what came through."

*With Jerry Reed and Fred in a scene from* Smokey and the Bandit

**B**urt has often been mentioned as being ideal for the kind of roles Clark Gable played back in the thirties and forties. Burt likes the comparison — what actor wouldn't — but he isn't one hundred percent certain, saying, "People never talk about Gable's gift for comedy, but the one time he won the Academy Award, it was comedy — *It Happened One Night*. Sure, I'd like an Oscar, and I hope I'm still around to appreciate it, if I ever do get nominated. I think my ability as an actor gets a little better each time out. Maybe that's why I keep working. I average two to three pictures a year, which is a lot these days. It may be heresy, but when I look at the pictures I do now like *The End* or *Hooper*,

*In* The End

they're miles ahead of *Deliverance* in terms of what I can do. But I guess I've been doing too many films that are similar to each other, and people take it for granted, the way they have always taken what Jimmy Stewart, for example, has always done. It's real work, making it look easy, but unless you've had to do it, you don't realize it."

On the subject of Clark Gable, when Burt was asked if he would have liked to have played Rhett Butler, he answered, "Oh yes, I would have loved that part. I was asked to play it in the sequel to *Gone With The Wind*, but I said I wouldn't play anybody who's still alive. They said, 'But Clark Gable is dead,' and I told

*In* The Fuzz

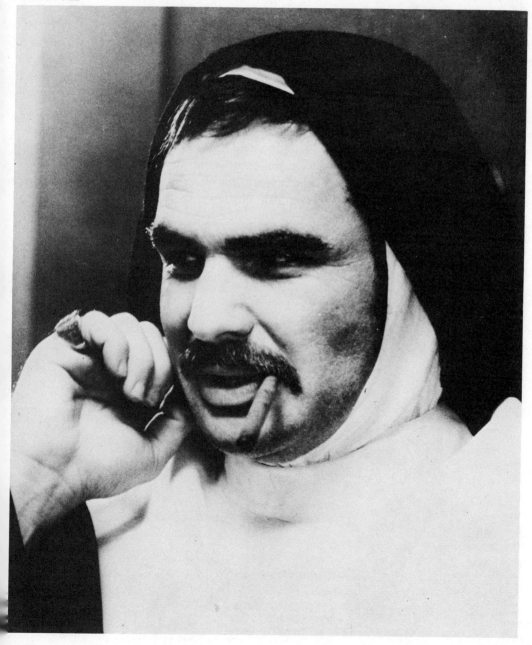

them, 'No, Hoot Gibson is dead. Clark Gable is still very much alive.'"

After talking about Gable, it would follow that someone was bound to ask him how he felt about Cary Grant roles, were he able to get the right scripts and directors. He said, "If I can be funny driving a car 100 miles per hour down a road, I think I can be funny in a drawing room wearing a dinner jacket and sipping a martini. I'd love to do a Neil Simon play like *The Goodbye Girl*. And I'm beginning to see more sophisticated scripts...."

Talking to Betty White for *Saturday Evening Post* Burt said, "I became a movie star not because of my image but in spite of it. I'm the only movie actor who has made hit after hit in spite of what the critics have written. Which doesn't thrill them. Once a critic wrote a review of *Smokey and the Bandit* that was longer than the movie. Anybody who would take that picture seriously needs a psychiatrist." When asked by Ms. White how it felt to make a crazy movie like *Smokey* and have it gross more than anything except *Star Wars* the year it came out, he replied, "It feels very good. Especially — and this rarely happens — because I did this as a favor to a stuntman friend of mine, Hal Needham, who had the chance to do this film. He sent me the script and I said, 'This is the worst script I have ever read, but I think we can make it work, if we get the right people.' Then we all sat down and contributed to it. After that it was fun and games, and the fun we had on the film was, I think, infectious to the American people who saw it."

The film was essentially one long wild and wacky chase. Burt was the "bandit" driving a Trans Am over every imaginable kind of terrain—over water, bridges,

bumpy roads and fields. It also included country singer Jerry Reed, who follows Burt in a huge tractor trailer loaded with an illegal cargo of beer. Then there is Jackie Gleason as a stereotyped Southern redneck sheriff, continuously on the verge of apoplexy, and finally, Sally Field, who plays the part of a runaway bride, who unexpectedly goes along for the ride. The picture was not a smash in the big cities, but it wowed them everywhere else as the box office receipts plainly indicated.

Perhaps, as Burt says affectionately, most of his audience climbs down from truck to see his movies, and perhaps get kidded a lot about the intellectual level of his films. But financially he has been very successful, commanding as much as $2 million plus a substantial percentage of each picture.

As an actor he knows exactly where he is and as a director he is very much coming into his own, both in the theatre and in motion pictures. Without making any noise about it, he has to date directed more than a dozen comedies for the stage and he intends to keep right on doing more. Despite an occasional turkey like *Lucky Lady* or *Nickelodeon*, he does what he wants to do because as he has proven, the secret of success is not liking what you have to do but doing what you like to do, because when you do it shows—and everyone else likes it too.

To an extent that explains why he still does his own stunts whenever he can. He says, "I do it because I enjoy it. It feels good coming out of something

*A scene from* Hooper                    *(overleaf) A scene from* Deliverance

physical. People like to equate stunting with a masculinity hangup. I don't agree. Besides, people don't really believe it anyway. Everybody thinks I'm an ass for doing my own stunts." Sometimes, like it or not, he can't do them. Investors in high-budget films get very nervous when the leading man is in danger of being incinerated, drowned, crushed or otherwise permanently put out of commission. There is little doubt, however, that he will continue doing them whenever he can.

One of the most radical departures from anything Burt ever did previously was the film *The End*, which he co-produced, directed, and played the lead in. It was a black comedy about a likeable man who is dying and who does not look forward to his imminent demise with anticipation, and who, in a moment of decision attempts to make arrangements to have someone do him in before he becomes bedridden.

On the surface it hardly sounds like a subject for comedy. But Burt had good reasons for choosing it. To begin with, he was tired of working on films where he had little or no control. Talking about *The End* he said, "It was originally written by Jerry Belson for Woody Allen, and it had been lying around for four or five years. Nobody would cast me in it, though I kept telling everyone, 'I should be playing this part, not Woody Allen.' Finally I decided to do something similar to what Sylvester Stallone did with 'Rocky.' I bought the script, produced it, and directed it, as well as being featured in it. The picture could surprise a lot of people who think I can only do limited things."

*Skulduggery*

There are many things in *The End* to upset many people. For example there is a sequence where Burt is given some less-than-adequate advice by a young, inexperienced priest. Those who missed the point regarded it as anti-Catholic, which it was not. In *The End*, Dom DeLuise plays the wacked-out loony who keeps trying to kill Burt because he sincerely believes he is doing his friend a favor.

Dom DeLuise's antic performance was highly acclaimed, especially in sequences where he goes through schizoid arguments with himself on the subject of helping Burt to kill himself. "Dom DeLuise ought to get an Academy Award nomination if there is any justice," Burt said, "which is a stupid thing to say. There is no justice!"

*The End* is far from one of Burt Reynolds' crowning achievements, either as an actor or a director. DeLuise was so outstanding in his clowning role that Burt at best, even though he was the lead, wound up as the straight man. But this didn't bother him at all, because after all, he was also co-producer and director. He compared *The End* to Woody Allen's second film, *Bananas*, saying, "This is not my *Annie Hall*, but it's a hell of a lot better than *Gator* [his first directing chore]. I want four or five films to show what I can do." And on the subject of acting he says, "I haven't done my best acting yet. So I'm not giving up acting to direct. I want to have the option to do both."

Quite clearly Burt has a lot of acting he plans to do, not to mention more stunting, as in *Hooper*, which was a tribute to the stuntmen he has known and

*Sally Fields in* Hooper

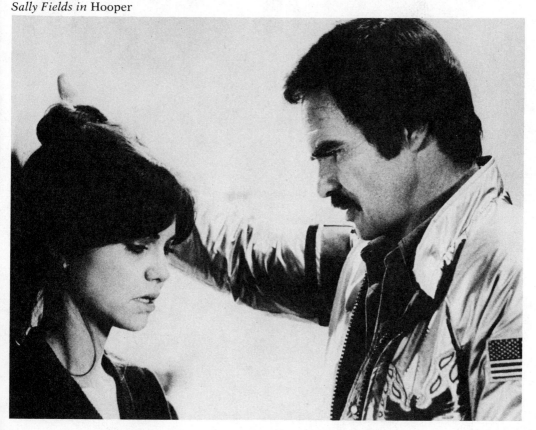

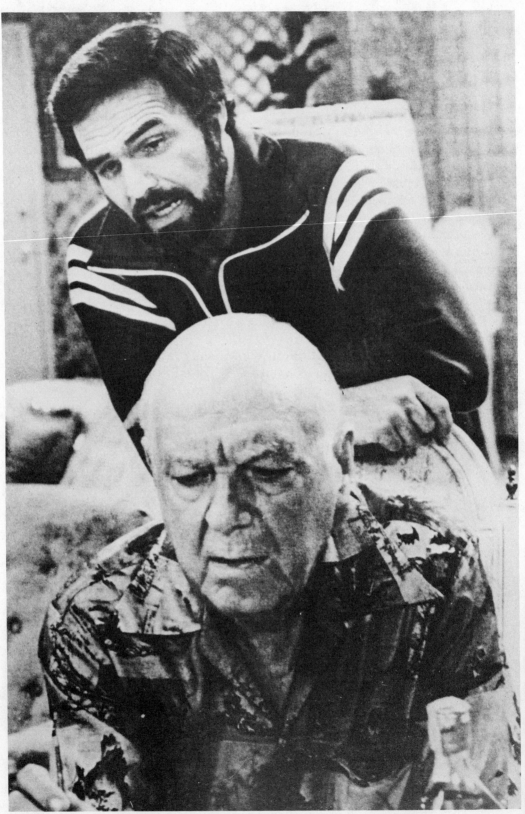

*With Pat O'Brien in* The End

worked with, and which was directed by his friend, Hal Needham. But it would seem safe to say that what has Burt most excited is his future as a director. He has said, "Directing was the most wonderful professional experience of my life, something happened to me that has never happened before. I didn't get tired. When acting, no matter how great the script or the role, I'm exhausted at the end of the day. But time literally flies when I'm behind the camera." Looking to the future he adds, "There is just so long that I can go on jumping out of windows, off cliffs, and over cars. I could walk away from the adulation I get as an actor and never miss it."

Though he has said that he would like to be like Jon Voight and wait for maybe five years between pictures until the right role came along, Burt knows that approach is not for him. As much as he likes directing, he still wants to improve as an actor. "I think the only way you can get better as an actor," he says, "is to act. I've been through enough bad television, bad movies, and bad reviews. I've paid my dues and then some. Now I'm going to take some chances." His most recent picture, Alan Pakula's *Starting Over*, is certainly one of Burt's chancier roles, for it is a complete switch. It is the obverse of Jill Clayburgh's *An Unmarried Woman*. In the film he gets dumped by Candice Bergen, a fact that will hardly cheer devotees of machismo, but he is hopeful and says, "I hope it will be my *Norma Rae*." Whether this proves to be the case or not, it is a safe bet to assume that whatever Burt has on the burners in the immediate future it is bound to do well, considering that in barely two years his films have grossed in the neighborhood of $400 million.

# N I N E

# BURT REYNOLDS ON BURT REYNOLDS

## ( AND OTHER MATTERS )

W atching how other humans behave is a great acting lesson. It's marvelous to watch bits of life unfolding. I used to love to go to bars and just sit in a corner and watch other people. Today people watch me. I go into a restaurant and everyone stares as I munch on my salad with some of it dripping down my shirt. I feel like a jerk."

"The saddest thing about getting to that age [40], is you start losing friends. They die all around you. People that you knew, loved, and cared for. Somehow it doesn't seem to happen when you're in your twenties and thirties. During the past year I've lost three close buddies, all of whom were older than me, but then again, most of my friends are. Friendship is the thing I treasure and cling to the most. I work very hard at friendships and am never prepared to accept an end to any of them."

"If someone suddenly took all my possessions away I really wouldn't mind except for one thing: my ranch in Florida; my mother and dad are there as well as my horses, and I just love the place. My friends all wear cowboy hats and have horse manure on their boots. They ask me if I knew John Wayne, and I say 'No,' and that's the end of the show business talk."

"I think it's important for an actor to save some of himself for the people he loves. If you go out and give everything of yourself, you have nothing left to make someone you love laugh or cry with you."

"I've got to have variety from now on. The trouble in Hollywood is that if you play a pink flamingo in a picture and it makes a lot of money, the next year all you get are pink flamingo scripts. But this is one flamingo that wants to be a 'gator, too."

"Being an actor is painful. Being a personality is painful. Being in the public eye in any way is painful. You can never give the public enough. They always want more."

"On the "Tonight" show 99% of all the leading men come on to talk about their pictures and their voices get a little lower, you know. They start saying, 'I loved the director, I loved the leading lady....' Before me, nobody ever came on and said, 'It's a turkey.' 'I've had an enormous amount of success doing that. People love it."

"There's more to life than being an actor. You get blinders about the business after a while. You think the only sunshine comes off reflectors; directing is different."

"The thought of dying doesn't bother me. I've had a fantastic life. Really fantastic. The only regret I'll have if something happened to me tomorrow is that I didn't prove to everybody that I was as good an actor as I think I am."

"Actually the only good thing about money is that I can now afford to turn down pictures that I don't want to make. Nobody seems to realize that I

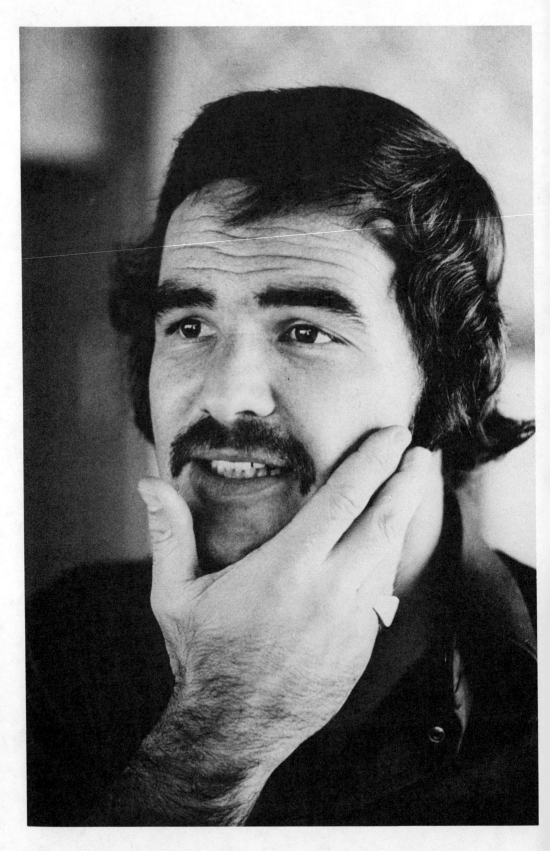

accepted a lot of lousy films in the past only because I wanted to improve myself. The money was incidental. I've always felt the only way to become a better actor is to act, and I think I've learned something with every picture."

"I've always been sorry I never finished college.... [At Harvard commencement] they were hoping for a Stanley Kubrick and they got this schmuck actor with a cowboy hat. When we were through we felt a mutual respect."

"Once I went into a restaurant with Orson Welles, and people came up to get my autograph. They completely ignored this phenomenal actor and genius beside me and I was really embarrassed. After they left, I apologized to Welles and he said, 'I have learned how to blend into the atmosphere. I can walk into a room and be completely unrecognized, but you—you stride into the restaurant like a peacock. No one can miss you.' I thought, *Lord, I hope not*. I wasn't even conscious of it. But now I can sometimes blend into the atmosphere, too."

"I admit I'm a flirt. I like women a lot—young, old, plain, pretty, any women."

"I have the feeling before diving into my swimming pool that someone is going to yell, 'Cut!' It's so unreal [in California], and I have never felt it was home. Now Florida is different and it can never get too hot for me. I never feel better than when I'm sweating profusely."

"I deal much better from a negative level. I'm much more articulate defending my work than praising it."

"I don't drink any more, don't smoke, and don't gamble. So I try to participate in as many activities as I can. The only thing I steer clear of is playing tennis with Chris Evert, because she's too good for me, and getting involved in politics. Most of my friends are very political, and they were chagrined when I wasn't active during the 1976 presidential campaign."

"I do things all the time that a movie star isn't supposed to do. I don't go to all the 'in' functions. And I appear on "Bowling for Dollars" or walk in on "The Carol Burnett Show." You're not supposed to do that. Nobody will come to see you, they say. Or, I go on the "Tonight" show and talk about how bad a film is."

"I don't get up in the morning and look in the mirror and say, 'Why aren't you married yet?' I'm just not ready. And there aren't that many good marriages around. I like to visit my mother and father every now and then because they have such a great relationship. I like to touch base and remind myself that it's possible to have a good marriage. I'll get married some day."

*With Lauren Hutton in* Gator

# BURT REYNOLDS'

# FILMOGRAPHY

1. **Angel Baby.** Allied Artists, 1961. Producer: Thomas F. Woods. Director: Paul Wendkos. Screenplay by Orin Borstin, Paul Mason, and Samuel Roeca. Adapted from *Jenny Angel* by Elsie Oaks Barber. (97 min.) **Cast:** George Hamilton as Paul Strand; Mercedes McCambridge as Sarah Strand; Salome Jens as Angel Baby; Joan Blondell as Mollie Hayes; Henry Jones as Ben Hayes; Burt Reynolds as Hoke Adams; Roger Clark as Sam Wilcox.

2. **Armored Command.** Allied Artists, 1961. Producer: Ron W. Alcorn. Director: Byron Haskin. Screenplay by Ron W. Alcorn. (99 min.). **Cast:** Howard Keel as Col. Mark Devlin; Tina Louise as Alexandra Bastegar; Earl Holliman as Sgt. Mike; Warner Anderson as Lt. Col. Wilson; Burt Reynolds as Skee; Carleton Young as Capt. Macklin; James Dobson as Arab; Marty Ingles as Pinhead.

3. **Operation CIA.** Allied Artists, 1965..Producer: Peer J. Oppenheimer. Director: Christian Nyby. Screenplay by Peer J. Oppenheimer and Bill S. Ballinger. (90 min.) **Cast:** Burt Reynolds as Mark Andrews; Kieu Chinh as Kim-chinh; Danielle Aubry as Denise Dalbert; Cyril Collack as Withers; Vic Diaz as Professor Yen; John Hoyt as Welles; William Catching as Frank Decker.

4. **Navajo Joe.** United Artists, 1967. Producers: Ermanno Donati and Luigi Carpentieri. Director Sergio Corbucci. Screenplay by Dean Craig and Fernando Di Leo. (Technicolor/Techniscope 89 min.) **Cast:** Burt Reynolds as Joe; Aldo San Brell as Duncan; Nicholetta Machiavelli as Estella; Tanya Lopert as Maria; Fernando Rey as Rattigan; Franca Polesello as Barbara.

**Shark!** Excelsior, 1968. Producers: Skip Steloff and Mark Cooper. Director: Samuel Fuller. Screenplay by Samuel Fuller and John Kingbridge from the book, *The Coral Are the Bones* by Victor Channing. (Eastmancolor 92 min.) **Cast:** Burt Reynolds as Caine; Arthur Kennedy as Doc; Barry Sullivan as Dan Mullare; Sylvia Pinal as Ana; Enrique Lucero as Inspector Biroc; Charles Berriochoa as Fatso; Carlo Borro as Runt.

6. **Fade In.** Paramount, 1968. Producer: Judd Bernard. Director: Jud Taylor. Screenplay by Jerry Ludwig and Mart Crowley. (Technicolor, 102 min.) **Cast:** Burt Reynolds as Rob; Barbara Loden as Jean; Patricia Casey as Pat; Noam Pitlik as Russ; James Hampton as Bud; Joseph Perry as George.

7. **Sam Whiskey.** United Artists, 1969. Producers: Arthur Gardner and Jules V. Levy. Director: Arnold Laven. Screenplay by William Norton. **Cast:** Burt Reynolds as Sam Whiskey; Clint Walker as O. W. Bandy; Ossie Davis as Jedidiah Hooker; Angie Dickenson as Laura Breckinridge; Rick Davis as Fat Henry Hobson; Del Reeve as Fisherman; William Schallert as Mint Superintendent Perkins.

8. **100 Rifles.** 20th Century Fox, 1969. Producer: Marvin Schwartz. Director: Tom Gries. Screenplay by Tom Gries and Clair Haufaker, from the novel *The Californio* by Robert McCleod. (De Luxe color 110 min.) **Cast:** Jim Brown as Lyedecker; Raquel Welch as Sarita; Burt Reynolds as Yaqui Joe; Fernando Lamas as Verdugo; Dan O'Herlihy as Grimes; Hans Gudegast as von Klemme.

9. **Impasse.** United Artists, 1969. Producer: Hal Klein. Director: Richard Benedict. Screenplay by John C. Higgins. (De Luxe color 100 min.) **Cast:** Burt Reynolds as Pat Morrison; Anne Francis as Bobby Jones; Clarke Gordon as Trev Jones; Vic Diaz as Jesus Jiminez Riley; Rodolfo Acosta as Draco; Lyle Bettger as Hansen; Miko Miyama as Mariko.

*With Michael Caine and Roger Moore in "Burt Reynolds in London"*

0. **Skulduggery.** Universal Pictures, 1970. Producer: Saul David. Director: Gordon Douglas. Screenplay: Nelson Gidding. **Cast:** Burt Reynolds as Douglas; Susan Clark as Sybil; Roger C. Carmel as Kreps; Paul Hubschmid as Van Cruysen; Chips Rafferty as Pops; Alexander Knox as Buffington; Pat Suzuki as Topazia; Edward Fox as Spofford; Wilfred Hyde-White as Eaton.

1. **Hunters Are for Killing.** CBS-TV, 1970. Director: Bernard Kowalski. (Technicolor 100 min.) **Cast:** Burt Reynolds as L.G. Florin; Melvin Douglas as Keller; Suzanne Pleshette as Barbara; Martin Balsam as Wade Hamilton; Larry Storch as Rudy; Jill Banner as Holly; Peter Brown as Raymond; A. Martinez as Ramirez; Ivor Francis as Carl.

2. **Run, Simon, Run.** ABC-TV, 1970. Producer: Aaron Spelling. Director: George McCowan. Teleplay by F. Siegel. (Technicolor 75 min.) **Cast:** Burt Reynolds as Simon Zuniga; Inger Stevens as Carroll Rennard; Royal Dano as Sheriff Tackaberry; James Best as Henry Burroughs; Rodolfo Acosta as Manuel; Herman Rudin as Asa; Eddie Little Sky as Santana.

3. **Fuzz.** United Artists, 1972. Producer: Jack Farren. Director: Richard A. Colla. Screenplay by Evan Hunter from the 87th Precinct novels by Ed McBain. (De Luxe color, 92 min.) **Cast:** Burt Reynolds as Det. Steve Carella; Jack Weston as Det. Meyer Meyer; Tom Skeritt as Det. Bert Kling; Raquel Welch as Det. Eileen McHenry; Yul Brynner as Deaf Man; James McEachin as Det. Arthur Brown.

4. **Deliverance.** Warner Brothers, 1972. Producer-Director: John Boorman. Screenplay by James Dickey from his novel of the same name. (Technicolor-Panavision, 109 min.) **Cast:** Jon Voight as Ed; Burt Reynolds as Lewis; Ned Beatty as Bobby; Ronny Cox as Drew; Bill McKinney as Mountain Man; Herbert Coward as Toothless Man.

5. **Everything You Always Wanted to Know About Sex (But Were Afraid to Ask).** United Artists, 1972. Producer: Charles H. Joffe. Director: Woody Allen. Screenplay by Woody Allen from the book by David Reuben, M.D. (Eastmancolor, 87 min.) **Cast:** Woody Allen as Fool/Fabrizio/Victor/Sperm; John Carradine as Dr. Bernardo; Lou Jacobi as Sam; Louise Lasser as Gina; Tony Randall as Switchboard; Lynn Redgrave as Queen; Burt Reynolds as Operator; Gene Wilder as Dr. Ross.

6. **Shamus.** Columbia Pictures, 1973. Producer: Robert M. Weitman. Director: Buzz Kulik. Screenplay by Barry Beckerman. (Technicolor, 106 min.) **Cast:** Burt Reynolds as McCoy; Dyan Cannon as Alexis; John Ryan as Col. Hardcore; Joe Santos as Lt. Promuto; Georgio Tozzi as Dottore; Ron Weyland as Hume.

7. **The Man Who Loved Cat Dancing.** MGM, 1973. Producers: Martin Poll and Eleanor Perry. Director: Richard C. Sarafian. Screenplay by Eleanor Perry from the novel by Marilyn Durham. (Metrocolor/Panavision, 114 min.) **Cast:** Burt Reynolds as Jay Grobart; Sarah Miles as Catherine Crocker; Lee J. Cobb as Lap-

chance; Jack Warden as Dawes; George Hamilton as Crocker; Bo Hopkins as Billy; Jay Silverheels as Chief Dancing.

18. **White Lightning.** United Artists, 1973. Producers: Arthur Gardner and Jules V. Levy. Director: Joseph Sargent. Screenplay by William Norton (De Luxe color, 101 min.) **Cast:** Burt Reynolds as Gator McClusky, Jennifer Billingsley as Lou; Ned Beatty as Sheriff Connors; Bo Hopkins as Ray Boone; Matt Clark as Dude Watson; Louise Latham as Martha Culpepper; Diane Ladd as Maggie; R. G. Armstrong as Big Bear.

19. **The Longest Yard.** Paramount, 1974. Producer Albert S. Ruddy. Director: Robert Aldrich. Screenplay by Tracy Keenan Wynn from a story by Al Ruddy. (Technicolor, 121 min.) **Cast:** Burt Reynolds as Paul Crewe; Eddie Albert as Warden Hazen; Ed Lauter as Capt. Knauer; James Hampton as Caretaker; Bernadette Peters as Secretary; Harry Caesar as Granville; Anitra Ford as Melissa Gaines.

20. **At Long Last Love.** 20th Century-Fox, 1975. Produced, directed, and written by Peter Bogdanovich. (Technicolor, 118 min.) **Cast:** Burt Reynolds as Michael Oliver Pritchard; Cybill Shepherd as Brooke Carter; Madeline Kahn as Kathy Krumm/Kitty O'Kelly; Duilio del Prete as Giovanni Spagnoli/Johnny Spanish; Eileen Brennan as Elizabeth; John Hillerman as Rodney James; Mildred Natwick as Mabel Pritchard.

21. **W. W. and the Dixie Dancekings.** 20th-Century Fox, 1975. Producer: Stanley S. Canter. Director: John G. Avildsen. Screenplay by Thomas Rickman. (TVC color, 91 min.) **Cast:** Burt Reynolds as W. W. Bright; Art Carney as Deacon; Connie van Dyke as Dixie; Jerry Reed as Wayne; Ned Beatty as Country Bill Jenkins; James Hampton as Junior; Richard D. Hurst as Butterball; Don Williams as Leroy.

22. **Hustle.** Paramount, 1975. Produced and directed by Robert Aldrich. Screenplay by Steve Shagan from his novel, *City of Angels*. (Eastmancolor, 118 min.) **Cast:** Burt Reynolds as Lt. Phil Gaines; Catherine Deneuve as Nicole Britton; Ben Johnson as Marty Hollinger; Paul Winfield as Sgt. Louis Belgrave; Eileen Brennan as Paula Hollinger; Eddie Albert as Leo Sellers; Ernest Borgnine as Santoro; Jack Carter as Herbie Dalitz.

23. **Lucky Lady.** 20th Century-Fox, 1975. Producer; Michael Grusskoff. Director: Stanely Donen. Screenplay by Willard Huyck and Gloria Katz. (De Luxe color, 118 min.) **Cast:** Gene Hackman as Kibby; Liza Minnelli as Claire; Burt Reynolds as Walker; Geoffrey Lewis as Capt. Aaron Mosely; John Hillerman as Christy McTeague; Robby Benson as Billy Webber; Michael Hordern as Capt. Rockwell.

24. **Silent Movie.** 20th Century-Fox, 1976. Producer: Michael Hertzberg. Director: Mel Brooks. Screenplay by Mel Brooks, Ron Clark, Rudy De Luca, and Bob Levinson from a story by Ron Clark. (De Luxe color, 88 min.) **Cast:** Mel Brooks as Mel Funn; Marty Feldman as Marty Eggs; Dom DeLuise as Dom Bell; Ber-

nadette Peters as Vilma Kaplan; Sid Caesar as Studio Chief. Guest Stars: Burt Reynolds, James Caan, Liza Minnelli, Anne Bancroft, Paul Newman, Marcel Marceau.

5. **Gator.** United Artists, 1976. Producers: Jules V. Levy and Arthur Gardner. Director: Burt Reynolds. Screenplay by William Morton. (De Luxe color, Todd-AO 35, 116 min.) **Cast:** Burt Reynolds as Gator McClusky; Jack Weston as Irving Greenfield; Lauren Hutton as Aggie Maybank; Jerry Reed as Bama McCall; Alice Ghostley as Emeline Cavanaugh; Dub Taylor as Mayor Caffrey; Mike Douglas as Governor.

6. **Nickelodeon.** Columbia Pictures, 1976. Producers: Irwin Winkler and Robert Chartoff. Director: Peter Bogdanovich. Screenplay by Peter Bogdanovich and W. D. Richter. (Technicolor, 122 min.) **Cast:** Ryan O'Neal as Leo Harrigan; Burt Reynolds as Buck Greenway; Tatum O'Neal as Alice Forsyte; Brian Keith as H. H. Cobb; Stella Stevens as Marty Reeves; Jane Hitchcock as Kathleen Cooke; John Ritter as Franklin Frank.

7. **Smokey and the Bandit.** Universal Pictures, 1977. Producer: Mort Engelberg. Director: Hal Needham. Screenplay by James Lee Barrett, Charles Shyer, and Alan Mandel from a story by Hal Needham and Robert D. Levy. (Technicolor, 97 min.) **Cast:** Burt Reynolds as Bandit; Sally Field as Carrie; Jerry Reed as Cledus; Jackie Gleason as Sheriff B. T. Justice; Mike Henry as Junior; Paul Williams as Little Enos; Pat McCormick as Big Enos.

. **Semi-Tough.** United Artists, 1977. Producer: David Merrick. Director: Michael Ritchie. Screenplay by Walter Bernstein from the novel by Dan Jenkins. (De Luxe color, 107 min.) **Cast:** Burt Reynolds as Billy Clyde Puckett; Kris Kristofferson as Shake Tiller; Jill Clayburgh as Barbara Jane Bookman; Robert Preston as Big Ed Bookman; Bert Convy as Friedrich Bismarck; Roger E. Mosely as Puddin; Lotte Lenya as Clara Pelf.

. **The End.** United Artists, 1978. Producer: Lawrence Gordon and Burt Reynolds. Director: Burt Reynolds. Screenplay by Jerry Belson. (De Luxe color, 100 min.) **Cast:** Burt Reynolds as Sonny Lawson; Dom DeLuise as Marlon Borunky; Sally Field as Mary Ellen; Strother Martin as Dr. Kling; David Steinberg as Marty Lieberman; Joanne Woodward as Jessica; James Best as Pacemaker patient; Jock Mahoney as Old Man. Guest stars: Robby Benson as the priest; Norman Fell as Dr. Krugman; Myrna Loy as Maureen Lawson; Kristy McNichol as Julie Lawson; Pat O'Brien as Ben Lawson; Carl Reiner as Dr. Maneet.

**Hooper.** Warner Brothers, 1978. Producer: Hank Moonjean. Director: Hal Needham. Screenplay by Thomas Rickman and Bill Kirby from a story by Walt Green and Walter S. Hendron. (Metrocolor, 99 min.) **Cast:** Burt Reynolds as Sonny Hooper; Jan-Michael Vincent as Ski; Sally Field as Gwen; Brian Keith as Jocko; Robert Klein as Roger Deal; John Marley as Max Berns; James Best as Cully; Adam West as Himself; Alfie Wise as Tony.

*Burt with his wax likeness at Movieland Wax Museum*

# SOME FACTS AND FIGURES

## Top Ten Box Office Stars: 1973 through 1978

### 1973
1. Clint Eastwood
2. Ryan O'Neal
3. Steve McQueen
4. **Burt Reynolds**
5. Robert Redford
6. Barbra Streisand
7. Paul Newman
8. Charles Bronson
9. John Wayne
10. Marlon Brando

### 1974
1. Robert Redford
2. Clint Eastwood
3. Paul Newman
4. Barbra Streisand
5. Steve McQueen
6. **Burt Reynolds**
7. Charles Bronson
8. Jack Nicholson
9. Al Pacino
10. John Wayne

### 1975
1. Robert Redford
2. Barbra Streisand
3. Al Pacino
4. Charles Bronson
5. Paul Newman
6. Clint Eastwood
7. **Burt Reynolds**
8. Woody Allen
9. Steve McQueen
10. Gene Hackman

### 1976
1. Robert Redford
2. Jack Nicholson
3. Dustin Hoffman
4. Clint Eastwood
5. Mel Brooks
6. **Burt Reynolds**
7. Al Pacino
8. Tatum O'Neal
9. Woody Allen
10. Charles Bronson

### 1977
1. Sylvester Stallone
2. Barbra Streisand
3. Clint Eastwood
4. **Burt Reynolds**
5. Robert Redford
6. Woody Allen
7. Mel Brooks
8. Al Pacino
9. Diane Keaton
10. Robert De Niro

### 1978
1. **Burt Reynolds**
2. John Travolta
3. Richard Dreyfuss
4. Warren Beatty
5. Clint Eastwood
6. Woody Allen
7. Diane Keaton
8. Jane Fonda
9. Peter Sellers
10. Barbra Streisand

# Burt On Records

## Ask Me What I Am.
Mercury. #SRM-1-693
**Contents:** *Childhood 1949, Slow John Fairborn, The First One That I Lay With, Till I Get It Right, She's Taken A Gentle Lover, You Can't Always Sing A Happy Song, Ask Me What I Am, A Room For A Boy Never Used, I Didn't Shake the World Today, There's a Slight Misunderstanding Between God And Man, I Like Having You Around.*

## At Long Last Love.
RCA Soundtrack. #ABL 2-9067
**Contents:** *Which?, Poor Young Millionaire* (Burt); *You're the Top* (Burt and Madeline Kahn); *Find Me A Primitive Man, Friendship* (Burt, Cybill Shepherd, Duilio del Prete, and Madeline Kahn); *But in the Morning, No, At Long Last Love,* (Burt); *Well, Did Ya Evah!* (Burt, Cybill Shepherd, Madeline Kahn, Duilio del Prete, and Mildred Natwick); *From Alpha To Omega, Let's Misbehave, It's De-Lovely* (Burt and Cybill Shepherd); *But In The Morning, No* (reprise), *It's De-Lovely/ Let's Misbehave* (Burt and Cybill Shepherd); *Just One Of Those Things* (Burt); *I Get A Kick Out Of You, Most Gentlemen Don't Like Love, I Loved Him But He Didn't Love Me, A Picture Of Me Without You* (Burt, Madeline Kahn, Cybill Shepherd, and Duilio del Prete).

## Lucky Lady
Arista/Soundtrack. #AL4069-0698
**Contents:** *Too Much Mustard, While the Gettin' Is Good, Christy McTeague, Young Woman Blues, The Guymas Connection/Dizzy Fingers, Lucky Lady Montage,* Medley: *If I Had a Talking Picture Of You/All I Do Is Dream Of You, Ain't Misbehavin'* (Burt); *Hot Time In The Old Town Tonight, Portobello Waltzes, When The Saints Go Marching In, Lucky Lady.*

## Zingers From The Hollywood Squares
(TV Soundtrack)
**Contents:** Burt Reynolds delivering one-liners from this television game show.

## Smokey And The Bandit.
(MCA/Soundtrack #2099.
**Contents:** *The Legend,* Incidental CB Dialogue (Burt and Jerry Reed); *West Bound And Down, Foxy Lady,* Incidental CB Dialogue (Burt, Jackie Gleason and Jerry Reed); *Orange Blossom Special, The Bandit, March Of The Rednecks, If You Leave Me Tonight I'll Cry, East Bound And Down* (reprise), Incidental CB Dialogue (Burt and Jerry Reed); *The Bandit* (reprise), *And The Fight Played On! My Cousin Plays Steel, Hot Pants Fuzz Parade,* Incidental CB Dialogue (Burt and Jackie Gleason), *The Bandit* (finale).

# Awards

1975 Golden Globe Award nomination for Best Actor in a comedy or musical—*The Longest Yard*

1975 Columbia Award for best actor—*The Longest Yard*

1978 People's Choice Award nomination, favorite actor

1978 NATO male star of the year

1978 *Photoplay* male star of the year

1979 People's Choice Award, favorite actor

1979 People's Choice Award, favorite all-around entertainer

# Acknowledgments

Without the previous hard work of others, this book could never have been written. They include: Joe Baltake, *Us, Current Biography*; Marilyn Beck and Robert A. Cutter, *Saga*; Joseph Gelmis and Pauline Kael, *New Yorker*; Bob Lardine, *Sunday News Magazine, New York*; Tammy Luft, *Rona Barrett's Hollywood*; Lois Armstrong, *People*; Edwin Shrake, *Sports Illustrated*; Betty White, *The Saturday Evening Post*; The NBC "Today" show, and my longtime friend, formerly of *Redbook*, Claire Safran. Finally, special thanks to another dear friend and veteran celebrity-watcher, editor and writer Seli Groves for the advice, time, and recollections. Substantial gratitude is also due to Philip De Lisi, a cinematographer-to-be and expert on Burt Reynolds. Without Philip's enthusiastic efforts in research, my job would have been measureably more difficult.